Scottish Mountaineering Club
District Guide Books

THE ISLANDS OF SCOTLAND

General Editor: MALCOLM SLESSER

DISTRICT GUIDE BOOKS

Southern Highlands
Central Highlands
Western Highlands
Northern Highlands
Islands of Scotland
Island of Skye
The Cairngorms
Southern Uplands

Munro's Tables

SCOTTISH MOUNTAINEERING CLUB

DISTRICT GUIDE BOOKS

THE
Islands of Scotland

by Norman Tennent

THE SCOTTISH MOUNTAINEERING TRUST

EDINBURGH

First published in Great Britain in 1971 by
THE SCOTTISH MOUNTAINEERING TRUST

Copyright © 1971 by the Scottish Mountaineering Trust

First Edition 1934
Second Edition 1952
First Edition New Series 1971
Reprinted with amendment 1976

Designed for the Scottish Mountaineering Trust by
West Col Productions

WHOLESALE DISTRIBUTORS
West Col Productions
1 Meadow Close
Goring on Thames
Reading Berks RG8 OAP

SBN 901516 47 3

Set in Monotype Plantin Series 110 and Grotesque 215
and Printed Offset Litho in Great Britain by Cox & Wyman Ltd,
London, Fakenham & Reading

CONTENTS

ILLUSTRATIONS

LINE DIAGRAMS

FOREWORD

THIS guide to the ISLANDS OF SCOTLAND is new. It is aimed not just at the mountaineer and climber, but at all who like to explore. Since Skye possesses two *S.M.C. Guides*, it and its adjacent islands of Raasay and South Rona are not included in the present work. Arran already has a detailed rock-guide, and so is here described only with respect to its mountains, together with some selected climbs.

The development of rock-climbing is now under way in the islands, where some remarkable faces are being discovered and some superb routes done. When the pace is so fast, a guide is bound to be out of date the moment it is published. Nevertheless, the reader of whatever sort he be, should find this guide most useful. Islanders have their own philosophy and pace of life, and islands demand from the visitor more than the passing glance of a tourist. The Guide Book Committee of the S.M.C. is fortunate in securing the services of Norman Tennent to rewrite the guide, for he brings the perception of a seafaring man as well as the intimate knowledge of the mountaineer to his writing. He has a unique knowledge of the seas and islands off the west and northern coasts of Scotland. The Committee is much indebted to him, and gratefully records its thanks.

Malcolm Slesser, *Glasgow, November 1970.*

ACKNOWLEDGEMENTS

LET me admit it. I cannot claim to have produced anything new or original on my own. Nor can I properly acknowledge all my debts because I can't remember when and where I incurred them. All I can do is accept with the best possible grace the help I have received on the way, knowing it cannot be directly repaid, but hoping to pass some of it on to others.

However, I know I owe a great deal to the diligent and resourceful Editors of, and contributors to, the earlier editions of this guide-book.

For their generous hospitality, and for showing no signs of the strain they must have felt during my frequent and protracted visits, I should like to thank the Slessers, the Andrew Arthurs, the Douglas Scotts, the Ken Johnstons, Eddie Thompson, Peter Mac-Donald, the good people of Harris, whose names I have forgotten, Captain Ross and the merry men of the 'Miranda' and many, many others. I should like to thank particularly W. H. Murray, T. Weir, H. MacInnes, A. D. S. MacPherson, C. R. Steven and D. C. Thomson for information and photographs.

I should also have liked to have taken this opportunity to have made some general but personal observations about the Guide Books General Editor, but since they would never have passed his scrutiny, I forbear.

INTRODUCTION

ISLANDS have always fascinated the human mind. Perhaps it is the instinctive response of man, the land animal, to the brief intrusion of earth in the vast overwhelming sea; to finding something tangible, on which he may make a mark in the midst of a great ocean, over which he may cross and re-cross, leaving no trace. He probably feels too, a sense of possessiveness he never knows in a great continent. If the island is uninhabited, he may be monarch of all.

The more inaccessible the island the greater the reward. To the climber who seeks the unusual and the unspoilt '*Il merit un grand detour*' as the *Michelin Guide* says. Though they may be mostly 'summer places' – the climber won't find great winter routes there – in the Islands late in the year the light and colour is unsurpassed, November is the month of lowest rainfall, and it is often possible to bask on a mountain-top in shirtsleeves at Christmas-time, or picnic on a sea beach at Hogmanay. In mid-summer he may find on the coast of an outlying island weather as rigorous as any he may encounter on a mainland summit.

No island should be written-off by the true mountaineer. It may look as flat and uninteresting as does Soay, for instance, from the superior height of the Cuillin ridge, yet turn out to have unique and fascinating traits of character on closer acquaintance. In following an island coastline, often shown with nothing of significance on a map, he is sure to find something of the same adventure and joy of exploration as in mountaineering, and have to employ some of the same skills and techniques.

To compensate for their lesser height, the islands have this rich, strange maritime quality to offer the mountaineer-explorer. Like the hot deserts, or the tundra of the Arctic, they turn out to be not barren but incredibly rich; and there is a purity about them in their primitive isolation, which they have managed to retain inviolate longer than the more frequented places of the earth. As Darwin noted: 'One of the most interesting and engaging characteristics of island species' – which here, might include man – 'is a lack of sophistication in dealing with the human race, which even the teaching of experience does not quickly alter.

'It is a curious pleasure,' he continued, speaking of the fly-catchers of the Galapagos that tried to remove hair from the heads of the men for nesting material – 'to have the birds of the wilderness settle upon one's shoulder. The pleasure would be much less rare were man less destructive.'

Though Highland hospitality is still as wholehearted as ever in places where the natives have not yet been overwhelmed by tourists, things will change all too quickly when the tidal wave brought by the new services and facilities, sweeps over them from the mainland.

As the pattern of island life is peculiar and significant, we should remember our obligations as guests, and not be too ready to impose our own standards. We should accept things as we find them, even if it means losing our hair.

History has constantly to be rewritten – slanted to new ideologies. The capacity to accept change and new ideas seems to signify a mature, developed intellect, yet it is also the trait of youth we should most wish to stay with. Old fallacies are bound to be perpetrated, and it is impossible to find a universally acceptable scale of importance. External factors, such as the weather, affect one's judgement. A cube, though exactly definable, must yet appear different to any one of several observers standing around it. And we have to acknowledge new authorities who are making history. In modern climbing those in the lead are far ahead; the lines of communication are becoming tenuous. We have to accept some of their reports without checking, for most of us are as likely to land on the moon or Mars as we are to scale the Old Man of Hoy or the Strone Ulladale overhang; a feature which is better seen, incidentally – is indeed quite beautiful – from a mile or two to the north-west. But it can never be the same again, for in our mind's eye there are men hanging like spiders beneath that fantastic roof. Some things were impossible when this Guide was first written; the ascent of the Ben Nuis chimney in Arran for instance, seemed the last word – but today we can't accept what even the top people say as final. According to W. H. Murray: 'The policy of the Scottish Mountaineering Club has always been to honour the mountaineer rather than the specialist; to encourage exploratory rock work and the art of route selection.'

Though we strive to improve routes and standards, and to learn from other climbers, provided the issue is to each individual to some extent in doubt, every climb is new.

As the greatest, latest problem which has just been solved in magnificent style is too extreme ever to be included in everyman's classics, our quest continues.

Grading

The grading of rock routes is done on the traditional, not the numerical system, namely: *easy, moderate, difficult, very difficult, severe, hard severe, very severe.*

Nomenclature

The Ordnance Survey spelling of place names etc., is used, except where this is not common usage, e.g.: 'Rhum' for 'Rum'.

The Scottish Islands in order of height

The heights given in the table which follows, and in the Guide generally, are from mean sea-level. Statute miles have been used, whether the distance measured is by land or sea, and 'true' bearings.

	ft.			ft.
1. Skye	3309	14.	Barra	1260
2. Mull	3169	15.	Borera (St. Kilda)	1245
3. Arran	2866	16.	North Uist	1138
4. Rum	2659	17.	Soay (St. Kilda)	1114
5. Harris	2622	18.	Ailsa Craig	1114
South Harris	1654	19.	Holy Island (Arran)	1030
Lewis	1885	20.	Ulva	1025
6. Jura	2571	21.	Scarp (West Harris)	1011
7. South Uist	2034	22.	Bute	911
8. Islay	1609	23.	Mingulay (Barra)	891
9. Scarba	1470	24.	Taransay	875
10. Raasay	1456	25.	Seaforth Island	713
11. St. Kilda	1397	26.	Canna	690
12. Scalpay (Skye)	1298	27.	Sandray (Barra)	678
13. Eigg	1289	28.	Pabbay (West Harris)	644

15

	ft.			ft.
29. Benera or Barra Head	631		42. Seil (Firth of Lorn)	479
30. Stac an Armin (St. Kilda)	627		43. Colonsay	470
31. Vatersay (Barra)	625		44. Soay (Skye)	462
32. Kerrera	617		45. Tiree	460
33. Eriska	609		46. Lismore	417
34. Dun (St. Kilda)	576		47. Great Cumbrae	417
35. Pabbay (Barra)	560		48. Benbecula	409
36. Carna (Loch Sunart)	553		49. Handa	406
37. Stac Lee (St. Kilda)	544		50. Little Cumbrae	406
38. Garbh Eilean (Shiant)	528		51. Tanera More	406
39. Muldoanich (Barra)	505		52. Sanda (Kintyre)	405
40. Gometra	503		53. South Rona	404
41. Muck	479		54. Arnamul (Mingulay)	403

Orkney and Shetland	ft.			ft.
Hoy	1565		Fair Isle	711
Shetland Mainland	1475		Yell	672
Foula	1373		Noss	592
Unst	935		Muckle Roe	557
Orkney Mainland	881		Westray	557
Rousay	821		Fetlar	521
Bressay	742			

Islands over 300 ft. include Coll (339 ft.), The Treshnish and the Garvellach groups (337 and 362 ft.). North Rona (355 ft.), Iona (332 ft.) and the Bass Rock (313 ft.).

The number of isles between 300 and 400 ft. above mean sea-level is 25, making 92 in all over 300. This includes Old Hill (off Loch Roag), 295 above high water springs, but not Flannan Mar or Oronsay. The height of Eilean Mhuire (Shiants, p. 93) is not known.

Access

Car ferry services operate from various points on the Scottish mainland to all the main islands or groups of islands. They form a network of systems independently serving:

 the Firth of Clyde from Gourock, Fairlie and Ardrossan,
  Mull   ,, Oban,
  Small Isles ,, Mallaig,
  Long Island ,, Uig, Skye,
  Orkneys and Shetlands from Scrabster and Aberdeen.

1. Arran, Glen Rosa from the air, looking north.

2. Cir Mhor from North Goat Fell.

Bibliography

Lists of books and works of reference are given at the end of each chapter. The S.M.C. rock-guides and current Journals are indispensable to those with serious climbing plans.

The first edition of this Guide was the work of the late W. W. Naismith, the founder of the Scottish Mountaineering Club.

First, for the latest, practical information W. H. Murray's *Hebrides* (Heinemann, 1966) and *The Companion Guide to the West Highlands of Scotland* (Collins, 1968) are admirable, and are works which no visitor to, or resident in the north should be without. Murray's *Mountaineering in Scotland* and *Undiscovered Scotland*, published by Dent, both have chapters on the islands. *The Island Hills* by Campbell R. Steven (Hurst and Blackett, 1955) deals with most of the inner Hebrides and conveys the particular charm and atmosphere of these islands. *Rambles in the Hebrides* by R. A. Redfern (Robert Hale, 1966) is also interesting as an individual's impressions.

It would be almost impossible to deal with the Niagara of books about the islands overflowing from the press. There are some not so recent works which if not yet 'classics' are well enough established to be respectable. *Island Going* by R. Atkinson is in this category, as is *The Book of Barra* by J. L. Campbell; likewise *Para Handy*, despite the attempt to make him into a TV 'classic'. Dr. Fraser Darling's *Natural History in the Highlands and Islands* (Collins, 1964) poses many interesting questions.

The West Coast of Scotland Pilot and the *Clyde Cruising Club Sailing Directions* are useful, dry though these nautical works of reference may be. *Cruising in the Western Isles* by John Maclintock (Blackie) is more chatty and diffuse, but still a good book to have beside the chart table. C. C. Lynam's *Log of the Blue Dragon* and Hugh Miller's *Cruise of the Betsy* (for its historical comment rather than sailing directions) should be mentioned for the benefit of the seafarer.

Sir Walter Scott, who, like Stevenson used the islands as the setting in some of his works, also went with the Light vessels around the north and west coasts. His passion was more for caves, dens, and ravines than for mountains. Yet William Daniell who dedicated his famous engravings in *A Voyage Round the Coasts of Britain* to Scott, depicted mostly mountains weird and wonderful though they may be.

Dr. John Macculloch was a contemporary and friend of Sir

Walter's. For the general reader his *Highlands and Western Isles of Scotland* (4 vols., 1824) can be recommended. It is very much concerned with the scene, which before had not been much noted. The work has an outstanding zest, and treats of practically every aspect of the country and its life: trade, timber, agriculture, music, antiquities, character, costume, customs and beliefs.

For a fairly modern adverse criticism of Macculloch see *The Book of Barra*.

Amongst early Victorian guide books and other curiosities may be placed Anderson's *Guide to the Highlands and Islands* of 1840, *The Steam Boat Companion to the Western Islands and Highlands* (J. Lumsden, Glasgow, 1820), and the *Souvenir Guide to the West Highland Railway Line*, published to commemorate the occasion when the Queen herself made the journey; though the only islands mentioned are Skye, Bute and Arran in passing.

Though Boswell's *Journal of a Tour to the Hebrides* mentions Skye, Raasay, Coll, Ulva, Inch Kenneth and Mull it is useless as a guide-book. The emphasis is shifted from the scene to the personality and person of Dr. Johnston. By his comments, disparaging and carping though they often were he often draws our attention to others, such as Martin Martin whose tastes and interests were different from his own. But of Thomas Pennant a Welsh squire who toured the Hebrides in 1772, Johnston said: 'He has greater variety of enquiry than any living man.' Indeed Pennant, who was a naturalist and an archaeologist and visited Bute, Arran, Ailsa Craig, Gigha, Jura, Islay, Colonsay, Iona, Staffa, Canna, Rum, Skye, Lismore and Scarba, filled in much of the picture that had hitherto been blank. A fine edition of Martin's *Description of the Western Islands of Scotland* of 1703, with all his maps and drawings was published by The Observer Press, Stirling in 1934.

Munro in his *Western Isles of Scotland* (1549) gave us the earliest written account we have of many of the islands.

To sum-up: Martin Martin, Macculloch, R. Atkinson, Seton Gordon, Fraser Darling, W. H. Murray, T. Weir and Campbell Steven seem to be the authors whose works must be on the essential list.

More specialised works which should be mentioned are: *Prehistoric Peoples of Scotland* by Stuart Piggott (1962) to be used along with the publications of the Ministry of Works, and Dr. A. Harker's *West Highlands and the Hebrides* (C.U.P., 1941) which describes what would be seen by a passenger on a steamer, and is the ideal work for a deckchair geologist.

The comprehensive transport guides and timetables *Getting Around in the Highlands and Islands* produced by the Highlands and Islands Development Board must be the best thing of the kind yet produced.

Amongst essential handbooks should be: *Flowers of the Coast* by I. Hepburn, *Sea Birds* by Lockley and Fisher and, to tell you what stung you *The Pocket Guide to the Sea Shore* by Barrett and Young; all published by Collins.

Natural History

The colonisation of the islands was accomplished by one of the strangest and most diverse migrations in earth's history. Carried by the wind, drifting with the currents or floating on logs, brush or trees, plants and animals arrived and established themselves.

So on the islands and around the coasts are found rare and charming plants and animals that elsewhere have retired to moors and remote mountaintops. Even the crumbling sandstone, shale or basalt cliffs, otherwise unattractive to climbers, are in the early part of the year transformed by blossom, into rock gardens of great beauty, all the more prized because they are rarely seen.

This migration began long before man appeared (he first came to the islands a lot later than he did to southern England): the evidence of it all lying in the raised beaches of Arran, Colonsay, Mull and Islay, the fossil beds and ancient kitchen middens.

It is thought that some of the western cliff edges escaped the last glaciation and that their pleistocene flora was not exterminated. Another part of the flora represents colonisation by sea along the sea-coast, from the Lusitanian region.

On the pages of more recent natural history man has written a black record. With the new insecticides he is exterminating many more primitive but interesting species, and with his indestructible detritus of the plastic age is fouling the sea and littering the beaches instead.

As Fraser Darling says of man's effect on the ecology of the islands: 'Seldom has he set foot on one but he has brought about disastrous changes, destroying environments by cutting, clearing and burning.'

Yet the inaccessibility of many islands still makes sanctuaries of them quite apart from those set apart for the purpose. In such places are to be found immense congregations of common, as well as rare species. The arctic fauna often overlaps the temperate, for example in its invasion from the north by whooper swans, great northern divers, Slavonian grebes and geese: and most recent and exciting of all – the snowy owls in Shetland.

Isolation has encouraged the evolution of local types. These, of which the Shetland wren and starling, the Hebridean hedge-sparrow, blackbird and song-thrush, the St. Kilda wren and house-mouse may serve as examples, are really part of a graduated system extending outwards from the mainland to the Faroes and Iceland. The local types of wrens for example, increase in size at a fairly steady rate of $1\frac{1}{2}$ per cent for every degree of north latitude. The question whether a local type is or is not a distinct variety is therefore of subsidiary interest.

The wildcat, the pine-marten, the badger, the red squirrel and the fox do not exist in any of the isles, except that there are foxes in Skye and badgers were introduced into Mull. Stoats are not found in the Outer Isles; weasels only in Islay, Bute and Skye. The blue hare exists on the more mountainous isles. In Mull there is the closely allied Irish hare.

Basking sharks are to be seen on their northward migration in May and June, and southward in September as well as the mammals, the porpoises and small whales. The Atlantic 'grey' seal breeds only in the remotest places, since unlike the common seal its young have to remain ashore for several months after their birth in October.

The principal species of sea-birds which throng the remote cliffs in spring and summer are gannets, fulmars, Kittiwakes, guillemots, razorbills, puffins, petrels, cormorants and shags. The increase and spread southward of the fulmar is of interest. Till near the end of last century St. Kilda was the only British breeding ground. There are only 21 gannet colonies in the world, of which the British Isles have about half. In the islands, St. Kilda holds one fifth, and Ailsa Craig, Sule Stack, Sulisker, Noss and Hermaness in Shetland and the Bass Rock the rest.

Weather

At Castlebay and Tiree respectively, strong winds (Beaufort scale 4 to 7) blow for 53 and 59 per cent of the time during the month of

April, and for more than two-thirds of the time in September, as compared with a sixth or a fifth of the time at Abbotsinch (Glasgow). The mean temperature for July is 56° F. at Tiree compared with 58° at Abbotsinch. The daily range of temperature is small in the isles: 9° at Stornoway and only 6° at Castlebay. It is 12° at Fort William and 13° at Abbotsinch. In Islay, Tiree or the Outer Hebrides the annual rainfall is between 40 and 50 inches; and on the coast of Mull or most of Skye, over 60. In the neighbourhood of mountains, there are still higher rainfalls, but much less than that in similar situation on the mainland. In the Western Isles, winds, particularly the moist ocean winds, assume great importance. They indicate a holiday in the early summer for dry weather. In Orkney and Shetland a rather later holiday for warmth.

History

The islands have their own special history, and the mountaineer may be presumed to be interested in the visible traces of history he may come on in his island wanderings.

The Dark Ages ended in the islands about the same time as the Middle Ages ended in the rest of Europe. In some remote islands they continued to the nineteenth century. The ancient strongholds used natural features in ways to interest the mountaineer who may re-enact history by storming ancient forts built to command defiles; or were observation posts on points of vantage on cliff-girt and barricaded headlands. Some were built on top of crags which cannot be reached without a scramble (Dun Canna, Brochel, The Pygmies Isle): on islets, occasionally artificial islets known as 'Crannogs': some only accessible by a submerged causeway with cunning traps for unwelcome guests or enterprising mountaineers.

Being less likely to be disturbed, islands were frequently used for burials. There are interesting carvings on crosses and headstones and slabs, as well as stone circles, huge burial cairns, imposing and puzzling brochs, underground dwellings, earth houses, 'Beehive Houses' (small hemispherical buildings cunningly roofed without the use of arches), tiny churches and hermits cells which give evidence of life and culture in places now desolate and deserted.

Lastly the traces of more modern ways of life; the sheilings or summer pastures on mountain slopes and high corries or islets still often used for grazing; the signs of clearances and desertion within recent times for which the Victorian/Edwardian sportsmen are culpable.

The difference between the tribes living south of the Forth and Clyde, and the Caledonians, living to the north, is reflected archaeologically in contrasting types of hill-fort, although very little other material is as yet forthcoming. Tacitus comments that the Caledonians were large and had reddish hair, and he compares them to Germans, presumably of the Celtic sort. This may be a factor in determining their origins, but their massive hill-forts, with stone and timber construction, would rather suggest a more immediate western starting-point, farther south along the coastlands of the British Isles. This, however, depends on the date of their arrival in Scotland; probably no earlier than the mid first century B.C.

It seems that in the first centuries B.C. and A.D. the Caledonian tribes had been able to choose the best region of Scotland in which to settle while, at a slightly later date, the British tribes, moving from south of the Cheviot, and the sea-faring migrants who built the brochs and wheel-houses, along the north-western and northern coasts and islands, had to be content with second-best. The Caledonian population included a strong indigenous, as well as an intrusive Celtic element. The language of the former was almost certainly not Indo-European, and the latter, while of the P-Celtic branch, was probably not identical with the form spoken by the British tribes.

The continuity between the Caledonians and the Picts appears to be well established. The Pictish Kingdom played its part in the formation of the historical Scotland. It is not certainly known what the Picts called themselves. 'Picti' is only used in written Latin.

Between the Roman occupation under Agricola, and the emergence of the Pictish Kingdom, Caledonian powers spread northwards and overcame the communities in the maritime archaeological province of brochs and wheel-houses. These subdued peoples were not important for later history, but the Orcades were certainly a Celtic tribe, and their name is still retained by their islands.

The Scotti, first recorded in the fourth century, with the Picts and a little later, the Saxons, all ravaged the Roman province. The name Scotti is almost certainly related to an Irish verb meaning 'to raid' or 'plunder'.

By the fifth century when the Kingdom of Dalriada was set up in Argyll and the neighbouring islands, settlement had taken the place of raiding. It was an off-shoot of the house of Dal Riada in north-western Ireland, and it was from this source, and no earlier than the fourth/fifth centuries, that the implantation of the Gaelic tongue progressively took place in Northern Britain.

After marshalling Celtic names in common use, study of the Celts should go no further. Thereafter it is a history of small kingdoms, in their fortunes one with another, and with the English, Norse and Normans. Inevitably the structure of Celtic society was lost. The survival of the languages came to rest on largely peasant populations, amongst whom might be seen the re-emergence of even more ancient ethnic groups overrun by the Celts.

The advent of Renaissance and exotic influences, however, coming in the train of the Christian missions, drew forth a responsive outburst of native excellence, both in the literary and manual arts. If Irishmen looked back to an heroic age, the saints and scholars had a Golden Age in their gospel books, precious metal-work, and the great sculptured crosses. The Celtic decorative motifs became but an undercurrent in the new art. At the great convention of Druim Ceat held in A.D. 575, St. Columba secured for the 'filid' their proper place in Irish life so that oral tradition and poetry were maintained.

The Scandinavian impact on Western Europe began through piracy. Wealthy monasteries like Lindisfarne and Jarrow were plundered and burnt in the last decade of the eighth century. These attacks were soon followed by settlement. Dicuil the Irishman, writing in c. 825, records that the Celtic hermits from Ireland had deserted the Faroe Islands because of the molestation of the Norsemen. The Irish annals note the sack of Iona early in the ninth century.

According to the Orkneyinger Saga, a Norse earldom, sprung from the Norwegian earls of More and nominally subject to the King of Norway, was established in Orkney rather before 900. The most powerful of this line, Earl Thorfinn the Mighty (*ob. c.* 1065), is stated to have held the Orkneys and Shetlands, the western islands and nine earldoms in Scotland. This represents the zenith of Norse power. The increasing strength of the crown led, in the course of the twelfth century, to the reassertion of Scottish sovereignty over the whole mainland. Norse sea power in the west was shattered at the Battle of Largs in 1263, but the northern islands remained a Norwegian possession down to the fifteenth century.

The Orkney and Shetland Islands, together with Caithness and the adjacent parts of the mainland, were thickly settled and became virtually Norse colonies; the same is probably true of Lewis. The western islands became and long remained a Norse possession, but the settlers were, in the main, an aristocratic ruling caste.

The picture of Norse settlement in the northern islands and Caithness is clearly shown by the many grave finds of pagan character.

Place-names tell the same story. The older toponymy of Orkney and Shetland is predominantly Norse and derived from western Norway. The long rectangular dwelling with the sides bowed outwards and the turf, stone-faced walls which appear in the earliest Norse farms at Jarlshof, on the Mainland of Shetland, find their best analogies in Iceland. The same type of dwelling is also known at Birsay, on the mainland of Orkney, at a period that can hardly be later than the ninth century.

The old Norse laws, in particular the odal rights in land, survived with modifications until the modern period, and the local Norse dialect, the Norn was still used in the islands in the eighteenth century. The only other area in which there is evidence for a similar change is the island of Lewis, which is thought to have been entirely Norse speaking in the eleventh century. All Gaelic names are relatively modern in appearance and very many of them are dated as post Norse by the Norse elements they contain.

Norse place-names occur throughout the western islands down to and including Arran. The proportion is highest in the Outer Hebrides, but except in Lewis, there is no reason to suppose that Norse speech entirely supplanted the local Gaelic. The archaeological remains in this area include a considerable number of rich burials. Ship burials with coins of Archbishop Sigmund of York (831–854) are recorded on the islands of Canna and Colonsay. A ship burial was also found on Oronsay, and the presence of boat rivets in the burial mound at Kingscross in Arran points to a further grave of that type. The rich ship burial indicates a man of high rank, a chieftain.

While in Orkney dedications show little or no trace of Celtic practice, a survey of the similar evidence in Islay reveals the continuity of the Celtic pattern of dedications.

The Report of the Royal Commission on Ancient and Historical Monuments deals with the Orkneys, Shetlands, Skye and the Outer Isles (including the Small Isles). It contains many photographs which are not otherwise available.

1

The Island of Arran

Ar – high, *Inn* – island.

The summits from south to north are:

Eastern Group:	**Goat Fell** (2866 ft.): **North Goat Fell** (2684 ft.): **Mullach Buidhe** (2688 ft.): **Am Binnean** (2172 ft.) on the east: **Cioch na h-Oighe** (2168 ft.).
Central Group:	**Beinn a'Chliabhain** (2217 ft.): **Beinn Tarsuinn** (2706 ft.): **Beinn Nuis** (2597 ft.) on the west: **A'Chir** (2335 ft.): **Cir Mhor** (2618 ft.): **Caisteal Abhail** (2817 ft.): **Ceum na Caillich** (2300 ft.): **Suidhe Fhearghas** (2081 ft.).
Western Group:	**Beinn Bharrain** (2345 ft.): **Mullach Buidhe** (2368 ft.): **Beinn Bhreac** (2333 ft.): **Beinn Bhreac,** north top (2305 ft.): **Meall nan Damh** (1870 ft.).

Maps: One-inch O.S., Seventh Series, sheet 66.
Half-inch Bartholomew, sheet 43.

ACCESS:

The main routes to Arran from the mainland are from Ardrossan and Fairlie, to Brodick. There are several car ferries to and from the former in the course of the day, and a full day can now be had on the island, using an early morning boat from Fairlie and one returning the same evening, with a connection by train to Glasgow. Time-tables are obtainable from British Railways, Central Station, Glasgow, or the Tourist Association Office, The Pier, Brodick, Arran.

Bus service timetables may be had from Arran Coaches, Brodick; and Bannatyne Motors, Blackwaterfoot.

CENTRES:

The best centre for climbers is Brodick. All the tops of the eastern and central groups can be readily reached from there. Corrie and Sannox are next best, but buses tend to run in accordance with boat times. A bicycle, which can be hired from a shop opposite the Post Office in Brodick, enables one to combine the advantages of both centres.

Pirnmill is nearest to the western hills, which may also be approached from Catacol and Lochranza via Blackwaterfoot.

Such is the popularity of the island during the holiday season that although practically every dwelling offers accommodation to tourists, difficulty may be experienced in finding any, unless booked in advance. There is a large camp site at the foot of Glen Rosa for tents and caravans. Further from the madding crowd, approximately two miles on up the glen, there are good campsites either side of the river. At the head of the glen, where the path starts to rise more steeply towards the Saddle, there are shelters, caves and 'howffs' conveniently situated for bivouacking.

General

The coast road is of interest as it runs on a 25 ft. raised beach, overlooked by the old sea cliffs and caves. The road which turns inland up North Glen Sannox crosses the continuation of the Highland Border Fault after about a mile. South from Lochranza along the west coast, the road follows the coast closely, and for 11 miles runs over Dalriadan shists (almost always on the 25 ft. raised beach) at a distance of $\frac{1}{2}/1\frac{1}{2}$ miles from the granite margin.

At the most northerly point of Arran – the Cock – there are several deep lateral chasms, which seam the hillside. Of the Cock, Anderson in his *Guide to the Highlands and Islands* (1850) says:

'Decapitation has impaired the resemblance it' (a boulder) 'used to bear to a cock flapping its wings'.

Lochranza he says: '— is a favourite rendezvous of the vessels and boats engaged in the Loch Fine fishery. The bustle of departure of an evening and of return with the spoils of the deep, and the operations of preparing fish for market – for most part in a fresh state – and shipping them on board the attendant buses contribute, during the fishing season, a peculiar interest to this otherwise retired spot.'

One is still conscious of the entity of this place through fishing with Kintyre, and the passage between, with twin forts guarding it at Lochranza and Skipness. From Campbeltown north along the coast of the Mull the graceful outline of Arran dominates all else, as a beautiful ship is better seen from some distance off than from on board her. One is too close to the hills when on the west coast of the island, to see them properly.

At the southern extremity of the island are the Struey cliffs. They have a large cave or excavation called the Black Cave, which is about 160 ft. long and has an exit at the rear. The area is a particularly good one for maritime plants, including some rarities. *Sorbus pseudofennica*, found only in Glen Catacol, along with *Sorbus arranensis* are two species of the White Beam Tree endemic to Arran.

Ways of access to the mountains are: from Brodick by Glen Rosa; from Sannox and Corrie by Glen Sannox (or directly from the coast road to the east face of Cioch na h-Oighe; from Lochranza by Gleann Easan Biorach; from Catacol by Glen Catacol, and from Pirnmill by the Allt Gabhlach.

Glen Rosa

A track, suitable for a Land-Rover, goes as far as the Garbh Allt bridge (not named on the O.S. map) over the stream that flows down from Coire a'Bhradain.

From Brodick onwards there is a fine view of the south-eastern part of the mountain tract, which consists of biotite-granite. The track is at first domestic and wooded. In the lower stages it is on old red sandstone for the first mile, then after crossing the Great Fault goes for a quarter of a mile over Dalriadan shists before reaching the granite. The Dalriadan rocks show best on Glenshant Hill on the east side of the glen. These rather uninspiring slopes (now relieved by a well-established larch forest) are, amongst the screes, good hunting-grounds for semi-precious stones. To the west, by contrast is the dark, forbidding eastern precipice of Ben Nuis, with its jagged skyline running north to Beinn Tarsuinn. They dominate the scene until the glen swings north and there is a magical change. One becomes aware of the perfect form and great charm of this island. The stream, running over the hard, vari-coloured granite seems to sparkle as nowhere else, even in dull weather. The shapely form of Cir Mhor and its setting as the focal point is unforgettable, and makes other famous views seem gross and inelegant by comparison.

To reach the Ben Nuis face, leave the track at this point shortly below the Garbh Allt bridge where a water-pipe bridges the burn. Follow the track branching left which climbs up the southern hillside to a small dam across the Garbh Allt, the tributary which joins the Rosa at the point where it turns north. Once across the burn head east-north east over gently rising moor into Coire a'Bhradain and thence to the subsidiary Coire nam Meann below the face. The central one of the five gullies which split the precipice is the notorious Nuis Chimney.

Glen Rosa from the Garbh Allt bridge on, where there are flat areas by the river bank on both sides, is boggy and wet. It would be difficult to reach the head of the glen dry shod, even in the driest summer. It is fairly heavy going until one starts to ascend more steeply towards the Saddle over into Glen Sannox, or the Fionn Coirre, to the west between the A'Chir Ridge and Cir Mhor.

From the Saddle (1413 ft.) the ridges to Cir Mhor and North Goat Fell rise to left and right. The sharp peak to the north (across the valley) is the Witch's Step, while to the east is the turreted façade of Mullach Buidhe.

Glen Sannox

The path starts at a hut some 200 yards south of the bridge over the burn at the village of Sannox. If the river is in spate, one may need to follow the north bank. Cross the stream to the north bank at the remains of a barytes mine. The glen (unlike Glen Rosa) is short and straight. Follow the north bank till the ground begins to rise towards the Saddle. The route then bears left up an easy scree gully. The ascent is steeper towards the top.

Suidhe Fhearghas on the right and Cioch na h-Oighe on the left mark the ends of the Central and Eastern Ridges. Seen from its lower end Sannox is wilder and more desolate than Glen Rosa, dominated by Cir Mhor's grand north-eastern face.

Anderson describes Glen Sannox as being: 'encompassed by spikey barriers of naked granite. It presents, in common with the adjoining glen, but perhaps in greater degree in its breadth of light and shade, its silent and unadorned grandeur, much of the wild solitude of the Cuchullins in Skye'.

Ridge Walks

The Arran hills are just sufficiently broken up to provide novelty and change of scene to sustain both the climber's interest and his height above sea-level. The going is so easy that it is possible to traverse all the main tops of the east and central groups in a day. It involves about 8500 ft. of climbing.

GOAT FELL (*Gaoth Bhein* – the hill of the wind, 2866 ft.)

The path from Brodick leaves the Corrie Road three-quarters of a mile after leaving the Rosa burn. It is well marked by signposts, then cairns up Meall Breac to the summit.

The route to NORTH GOAT FELL (near O.S. pt. 2659) gives good scrambling if the castellated tors are climbed. Sheep tracks lead either side of these.

To reach THE SADDLE follow down the narrow ridge towards Cir Mhor.

Beyond NORTH GOAT FELL the main ridge is wide; after a col, some towers may be skirted on the left or avoided on the open slope on the right. Before the summit of MULLACH BUIDHE (2688 ft.) is reached a subsidiary ridge, ill-defined at first, leads out to AM BINNEIN. From the north slope of the summit plateau springs two ridges which enclose Coire na Ciche (Devil's Punch Bowl). The left hand one leads to CIOCH NA H-OIGHE (the maiden's breast, 2168 ft.) and so down to Sannox.

THE CENTRAL RIDGE

The traverse from BEINN NUIS to SUIDHE FHEARGHAS is one of the finest mountain walks in Scotland, though the distance between these summits is under five miles.

From Brodick take the track leading up Glen Rosa to the Garbh Allt pipeline, then up the south bank of the stream, crossing it below the dam to reach the moor and the south-east shoulder of the mountain as previously described.

BEINN NUIS (the face mountain, 2597 ft.)

The fine cliff, 500 ft. high, which flanks the hill on the east is the chief object of interest. The traverse of BEINN NUIS is easy, though it is possible to mistake the south-west for the south-east ridge in a mist. The route to BEINN TARSUINN lies across gentle grassy slopes in a north-easterly direction, skirting the cliffs.

BEINN TARSUINN (the transverse mountain, 2706 ft.)

The view from this peak is very extensive. Particularly fine from this aspect is GOAT FELL and its serrated ridge leading northward to CIOCH NA H-OIGHE, while to the west is a contrast in the rounded forms of the western hills and desolate glens and moorland.

On the descent to Bealach an Fhir–Bhogha (pass of the bowman), which lies between Glen Iorsa and Coire a'Bhradain, any difficulties can be avoided by keeping to the left – the west – side.

BEINN A'CHLIABHAIN (the hill of the sword, 2217 ft.) – comes

in at this point from the right (east). It is most easily ascended from Glen Rosa by its south ridge.

A'CHIR RIDGE rises north from a col (2106 ft.)

The ridge can be entirely avoided by a path low down on the Glen Iorsa (west) side to reach the crest of the ridge again at the A'Chir–Cir Mhor col (1933 ft.). A'CHIR summit can be reached from its eastern shoulder from Fionn Coire, turning the lower summit on the south, and so up the summit boulder.

To follow the crest of the ridge is the best scramble on the island. It is probably more difficult going from north to south than the other way.

From the south end to the summit several routes are possible from an easy scree gully on the Iorsa side to scrambles near the crest and hard rock climbs on the east face. The northern section of the ridge after the summit is the more interesting and has some fine situations, including a tricky descent on the Iorsa side to the 'impassable' 'mauvais pas', a 15 ft. wall, and a traverse along an exposed ledge across the east face.

CIR MHOR (the great comb, 2618 ft.)

From the A'Chir–Cir Mhor col to the summit is merely a steep walk. It affords, however, spendid views of the Rosa Pinnacle, Cubic Ridge, and other features of the south face. It is one of the sharpest tops in Scotland. The views all round are splendid, the absence of CIR MHOR itself being the only thing that is lacking.

The ascent over steep grass, heather and scree can be made from the Saddle in under an hour.

CAISTEAL ABHAIL (Ptarmigan's Stronghold. 'Castles' 2817 ft.)

From CIR MHOR one has to partly retrace one's steps towards A'CHIR then turn north towards the col (2046 ft.). There is a spring marked by a cairn – the time-honoured luncheon place – 400 ft. below the summit. The rock architecture of the north face of CIR

MHOR looks particularly fine from this point. The summit is the second highest and perhaps the best viewpoint in Arran. It has four ridges leading from it. The summit towers of which the central is the highest, a semi-circle. There is another top to the north-west (2735 ft.) and a long ridge leading in the direction of Lochranza. A shorter, steeper ridge descends north into North Glen Sannox. The east ridge leads, after the descent to a level section crowned with tors and a loose section down to the gap before.

CEUM NA CAILLICH (The Witch's Step or Carlin's Leap, 2300 ft.)

The ascent from the gap is by a sloping slab, angled at about 30°, moderate in standard followed by a scree gully. At the top go right into a cleft, then out and across it at the top, to the summit boulder. All complications may be avoided by descending north from the east ridge of CAISTEAL ABHAIL, and on reaching the corrie floor, follow a path which ascends gradually to the Suidhe Fhearghas saddle. There is a good echo across the gap, said to be useful for finding one's directions in a mist.

SUIDHE FHEARGHAS (Seat of Fergus, 2081 ft.)

This is the northernmost summit on the central ridge. Its ascent from the col is gentle. The descent from the summit to Glen Sannox is steep, rough and heathery.

King Fergus the First is said to have ascended this hill to survey his Kingdom. At the top he sat down to dine in state. The modern climber with no attendant commissariat has to wait till he has descended to sea-level.

THE WESTERN HILLS are readily reached from Pirnmill. They are of a fine-grained granite that has weathered faster than its coarser neighbours to the east. BEINN BHARRAIN, the highest summit of the group, is best ascended by its north-west ridge which lies $1\frac{1}{2}$ miles east of Pirnmill. It is well-defined and gives some scrambling.

From Catacol and Glen Catacol, MEALL NAM DAMPH (1870 ft.) can be reached, and thence along the ridge to BEINN BHREAC (Spotted Hill 2333 ft.). In Coire an Lochain, on its north side, is the only genuine mountain lochan in Arran. From BEINN BHREAC the ridge continues to BEINN BHARRAIN (barren mountain 2368 ft.). The south top (2345 ft.) consists of two tors, in one of which is a tunnel. It is four miles from the summit to the coast road at Dougrie Lodge.

It is possible to traverse the island after ascending this group, after

31

crossing Glen Iorsa, either passing south of CREAG NAN MEANN and BEINN NUIS or crossing the bealach between CHIR MHOR and the A'CHIR ridge (1933 ft.). The moor consists largely of tufty, ankle-twisting grass, but the wild-life, both flora and fauna, is abundant.

Rock Climbing

Whether from afar, the middle distance, or close-to, Arran is an agreeable place for the climber. The ridges provide enough technical difficulty to please the young and innocent as well as the more staid and experienced. It has great rock routes whose particular quality is unlike anything else. However, Arran rock offers little choice between easy to moderate scrambles and hard, strenuous routes. One should not be deceived by the angle of a face into thinking it will be easy.

The Scottish Mountaineering Club has published *Rock Climbs in Arran* (W. Wallace, 1970) which details all climbs. As Arran is very much a 'summer place' we make no apology for infringing on the other's province, and including some of the best rock climbs. It would be wrong to think of Arran as a mere practice ground for bigger things – a probable error made by many who spent formative years or had early associations with the island.

CIR MHOR

The greatest and most important route is the *South Ridge Direct* of the Rosa Pinnacle, 855 ft., Very Severe. It is considered among the best anywhere in the country. One should choose a sunny day to savour its delights to the full.

From Fionn Coire (reached from Glen Rosa) one can pick out the elongated S-crack running up the otherwise flawless vertical nose of the ridge which rises out of a jumble of slabs. The climbing really begins at a conspicuous rock crevasse 60 ft. below and some way to the right of the S-crack, level with the jammed blocks in Sub Rosa Gully. This point is best reached by an ascending traverse over slabs from the left (200 ft. approx.) or more directly by a steep groove near Sub Rosa Gully. The S-crack is the second pitch (40 ft.) and the most strenuous. The harder Y-crack above it may be avoided by a delicate right traverse (a wedged nut and sling may give doubtful

3. Arran ridges, looking east over the Carlin's Leap and Castles to Cioch na h'Oighe and Goat Fell.

4. Cir Mhor and the North-East corrie.

5. Davaar Island, Campbeltown Loch.

6. Bute and Arran from Loch Striven.

security) and up a vegetatious gully. The climb continues up slabs to a block-strewn terrace. A traverse left across the top of a great slab leads to a side belay in the far corner. From here layback up the flake crack and then make a delicate traverse rightwards across the foot of the upper slab until it is possible to move upwards to the wide platform above.

Fig. 1   CIR MHOR   *South Face*

1. Sou-wester Slabs
2. West Flank Route
3. South Ridge Direct

4. Sub Rosa Gully, for
   Labyrinth and other routes on
   East Face of the Rosa Pinnacle

A chimney above, easy rocks and a level ridge lead to the Terrace and the Upper Pinnacle. There are several more pitches to the climb. Though the standard is little more than difficult, the situations are very fine.

This route was a landmark in the history of Arran climbing. J. A. Ramsay and party climbed the original route in 1933. It started at the foot of Sub Rosa Gully and involved a scramble up a grassy gully to a nook. There were three pitches. A rope from above was

33

used for the 'Layback' Crack. The same party did the complete climb in 1935.

J. F. (Hamish) Hamilton and G. Roger attempted the Direct Route in 1940, but avoided the S-crack by a rightward traverse, finishing up Original Route. In 1941 Hamilton and D. Paterson climbed the S-crack and the twin cracks with their final overhang.

In 1945 R. K. Fraser and party gained the foot of the S-crack by severe climbing on the left of the usual route. Though somewhat artificial, this probably accords best with the character of the succeeding pitches.

Of more recent importance is *Bluff* 250 ft., Very Severe, H. Donohoe and E. MacLellan, 1968, which goes directly up the front of the upper pinnacle. It seems certain that this route will become the direct finish to the South Ridge Direct, maintaining as it does the standard and excellence of the lower part.

Labyrinth – (350 ft., Very Difficult, strenuous). Also on the Rosa Pinnacle, but different from the South Ridge in character. (Formerly called East Wall.) The start is well up the gully to the east of the Pinnacle, the Sub Rosa Gully. Route finding provides no small part in the interest of the climb: a guide-book-in-hand climb. Ascending the gully the first break in the East Wall is a vertical chimney. Higher is a terrace running up steeply from left to right. Climb a chimney which cuts into the terrace, taking the right fork at the top. Ascend to a corner and gain the top of a large block. A grassy groove on the right eases to a grass shelf: go left, across a steep wall by a hand traverse. Continue upwards for 150 ft. mainly in chimneys to a point 50 ft. below the summit ridge. A long ascending traverse right and a short chimney at the north-east corner of the Pinnacle lead to the summit.

On the opposite – the west – side of the Rosa Pinnacle is one of the most pleasant climbs on the island – *Sou-wester Slabs* route – a long, Very Difficult slab climb with splendid situations, and West Flank Route, said to be the plumb of the decade; certainly not a chestnut. (See the remarks following on North Face routes.) It follows a natural line of chimneys, cracks and grooves, and starts in a very obvious tapering two-tier chimney which leads obliquely up to the left. The climb is strenuous, particularly at the beginning. The final move on pitch 3 needs care when water seeps on to the slabs; dry conditions are desirable. Pitch 4 might be straightened out by a delicate but feasible looking traverse.

On the opposite side of the mountain from the Rosa Pinnacle, the North Face which overlooks Glen Sannox, is truly impressive from any viewpoint. It seems to promise many fine long routes, and any climber 'pioneering' must be drawn to it as a moth to a candle. However, not one first-class route has been found on the entire face. As proof of its continual fatal attraction we quote from, first – The *1966 S.M.C. Journal* in which P. Brian and R. Campbell refer to their route, which they call *Ribbish* as being on 'the rib to the left of B-C Rib, bounding the lower North-East face on the right. The description is included to spare other would-be pioneers its loose and slimy horrors. An appalling climb fraught with objective danger and continually unpleasant'. Then a note by the Editor appeared in the *1967 Journal*, stating – 'This marvellous plum – *Ribbish* – was picked in 1903 by Messrs. Goggs and Bennet-Gibbs. A chestnut.'

B2-C Rib, *Bow Window Cave* and *Bell's Groove* probably provide the most satisfactory sequence up the face.

BEINN NUIS

As it must be mentioned somewhere, perhaps here we may go back in history and to the south end of the mountains, to the in-famous Chimney on Beinn Nuis, and the best thing about the climb is the account of its first ascent in 1901 by E. A. Baker and party in *The British Highlands with Rope and Rucksack*. He wrote a classic account of what can never be a classic route.

On the first pitch (their) 'leader by patient and plucky efforts won his way up, and was loudly cheered by us and by the friends watching from the fell-side. He managed to secure a grip, a sorry and doubtful grip it was, by standing on Oppenheimer's shoulders, who in turn was propped and steadied by me.' (Nowadays one is advised to drive blade-type pegs into a crack on the right, and with slings or étriers conquer the bulge). 'Oppenheimer then held his foot while he struggled upwards an inch at a time, digging his toes into the mossy channel and spreading himself out so as to utilise every particle of friction. . . . From below the rocks belied their nature. What looked like a handy knob proved to be a rounded corner impossible to grasp; it was so all the way up' – and so on. For a modern assessment of this route see the *Arran Rock Climbing Guide*.

The climb was not repeated until 1955. It was found then to be perfectly safe and feasible to keep in the chimney all the way; the first ascent involved several excursions on to the dangerous faces flanking the fissure. A prolonged dry spell and a supply of blade-type pitons are required for an attempt on this route.

W. H. Murray's account of his ascent of the three recommended routes on the North Face of Cir Mhor is another classic. In *Mountaineering in Scotland* he says – 'Many years ago in a paper read before the Alpine Club [he was writing in 1939] this rib (*B2-C Rib*) has been described as the most dangerous of Scottish rock climbs, mainly, I think, on account of the paucity of belays', and – 'we came to a tilting grass platform, and there, hard before us, sprang the great slab which had drawn my suspicious eye from the corrie.

'The pitch was an unbroken sweep of granite, shield-shaped, bare of feature save for one long groove, too thin for hold, which ran diagonally from the low left to the top right corner. In this shallow score were lodged at intervals a few tufts of coarse grass, whose cushion might accommodate the edge-nail of a boot. . . . Nothing would persuade me to venture on it in wet weather.' So to the overhang – 'I edged out to the right on small notches, taking my handholds low down to preserve arm strength, then went straight up until the overhang stopped me. At this vital point I found an undercut hold at waist-level, on which I was able to lean out of balance and stretch the left hand over the top. My hurriedly groping fingers at once closed round the ideal handhold, the same that has ever charmed my dreams, but which never till now materialised in the living rock – a jug handle. One vigorous pull up and my chest was over the brink, legs dangling in thin air; then with a few press-holds I pushed myself up to the easy rocks beyond. Like many an impending obstacle in life, it fell at once when boldly tackled; and the joy of swarming over this brow of space was out of all proportion to the technical difficulty. One's blood spins and the spirit sings. No melancholy in a man can survive such rock' – or morbidity either: feats of acrobatics were performed in the *Bottle Dungeon Route* which is one of the usual finishes to B2-C Rib.

They finished by *Bell's Groove*, of which he says – 'A great slab is cleft by a diagonal crack. I recall no definite holds. The friction of cloth and skin and the jamming of the right boot in the crack were the means of adhesion and propulsion.'

BEINN TARSUINN at the south end of the A'Chir Ridge has, on its Meadow face several noteworthy routes. The feature lies at the head of Ealta Coire above a pleasant patch of gravelly turf (the Meadow).

Slabs rise from the Meadow, and above them is a wall which is vertical for 200 ft. at one point. Left of this are two face-cracks widening into gullies high up; the left is Hanging Gully. To the right of the vertical wall is a fan of ledges; next the angle eases and three cracks run up the face (Meadow Grooves).

Brachistrone is a fine climb affording sustained difficulty and remarkable situations particularly in its lower half. Under the prevailing wet conditions, when it was first climbed, it was found to be a comparable undertaking to The Bat on Ben Nevis and it seems unlikely that it would be found much easier in completely dry conditions.

On the southern side of the face there are two parallel cracks leading directly to the summit of the buttress. The route follows the left hand crack.

The other two recommended climbs on this face, apart from *Brachistone* (MacKeith and M. Galbraith, 1966) are *Bogle*, 820 ft. (I. G. Rowe and I. Dundas, 1967) – the third of the long parallel cracks – and the *Rake* (W. Skidmore and R. Richardson, 1962). These three routes are amongst the best in Arran to date. They are similar in standard, difficulty and quality (Very Severe and A2).

CIOCH NA H-OIGHE, the mountain at the north end of the Eastern group has a steep eastern face which looks promising. It is, however, similar to the North face of Cir Mhor to some extent. The rocks are very vegetatious, and are slimy and wet in bad weather. There is, however, a feature known as the Bastion, a section of sheer rock, which lies directly below the summit on the East face. It is very prominent from the Sannox–Corrie road. It provides the best route to date on this face and is of high technical interest and position. It is called the *Klepht* – (300 ft., Hard Very Severe). It follows a great crack, the main weakness up the front of the Bastion.

Tidemark, a 360 ft. Hard Severe route done by A. Maxfield and J. Peacock on 9th June, 1960, follows an obvious gangway round the upper part of the Bastion and starts at a good spike-belay just above Ledge 3, about 200 ft. from the ledge's upper end.

North Glen Sannox has recently provided one or two routes. It has the merit of being not much frequented as a development area, but transport may be a difficulty. The routes are on the east face of the ridge dividing Coire nan Ceum from the corrie to the west (O.S. reference 453969). All are routes of very severe standard of two to three hundred feet.

TOR NEAD AN EOIN – lies 1½ miles south-east of Lochranza. The rock face on the west side is interesting geologically, the northern part being schist and the southern part granite. The latter is too broken-up for climbing, but the former is of considerable interest. It is steep and the exposure considerable. The rock is generally sound but lacks natural belays. The crag is totally different from anything else on the island, and being low (1½ hours from the road) is often dry when the other crags are mist-fast and wet.

The schist face, about 250 ft. high and triangular or pyramidical in shape, is bounded on the north by broken ground and on the south by a messy gully – *Verdant Gully*. Immediately north of the gully and cut off from the main face by a diagonal grassy rake is a large tower about 150 ft. high, teeming with overhangs. There is an evasive mild very severe route up this tower. The main face lying north of the tower has the following principal features:

(1) A deep groove running from bottom right to top left, the line of the original route – *Aquila*, and the best line on the crag. It continues up to an open groove which leads to a grass ledge. Continue up the groove (severe) or traverse left until a line of weakness gives access to the slabs higher up (very difficult).

(2) A grass terrace across the face 70 ft. up.

(3) A belt of overhangs about 30 ft. up.

Grey Wall route starts at the lowest and steepest part of the slab and continues to a prominent overhang, where one moves left to a shallow groove.

To commend these routes is their remoteness from Brodick, which as a centre for climbers, is usually too full of people who are not.

BEINN BHARRAIN

There are one or two routes on the craggy east side of a ridge coming from the north (map reference 898429). Half-way across the crag is a buttress with an obvious crack running from bottom right to top left. Start at the crack and traverse left at top for 20 ft. then up 10 ft. wall.

A right-angled corner, a crack in a 40 ft. to the left of the preceding route, gives a Mild Very Severe route of about 200 ft.

MAOL DONN (1208 ft.)

For those seeking a change from granite and a way of spending an afternoon that might otherwise be wasted, there is sandstone about 2 miles south of Corrie on the north face of Maol Donn. (For an impressive photograph see The Photographic Supplement of Stanford's Geological Atlas.) The cliff rises to 1200 ft. and the stone was once quarried for building purposes. It is false-bedded Eriassic sandstone, according to W. Gunn of the Geological Survey. The principal route lies up a deeply cut chimney, 100 ft. high; difficult in standard. As such lines in such rock are not of the best, an open face approach may be more rewarding.

HOLY ISLAND

The mouth of Lamlash Bay is almost blocked by the steep-sided Holy Island making it one of the finest natural harbours in the British Isles. During the last war it was used as a base for the Atlantic fleet. It rises to 1030 ft. in Mullach Mor and wild goats roam the steep slopes, the western being of tiers of porphyry and claystone which yield some sport to those enterprising enough to visit the place. The standard approach is by swimming across the channel from King's Cross Point (severe for moderate swimmers). It is possible to hire the services of a boatman at Kingcross village, near the Point (map reference 056284). A very interesting day can be spent on this island. The name comes from the fact that in the sixth century St. Molaise, one of Columba's disciples, lived here to the extreme age of 130. His cave, with its preaching stone and a spring of water can be seen just above the path on the western coast (map reference 059297). There is the site of an ancient monastery near the farm at the south-eastern corner of the island.

PLADDA

The island of Pladda is separated from the extreme southern tip of Arran by a mile of often turbulent water. It can be reached from Kildonnan (map reference 233208). From Kildonnan a submerged reef runs out to Pladda to which boats keep to the eastern side. Pladda is less than half a mile from north to south and quarter of a mile from east to west. It barely reaches 40 ft. above sea-level. The light was not extinguished during World War II, so useful was it to our ships making the landfall from the west. On the island may be seen seals, gannets from Ailsa Craig, common terns, small groups of Arctic terns nesting, shelduck, red-breasted merganser and corn-crakes occasionally on migration.

REFERENCES

Description of the Western Isles of Scotland, Donald Munro, 1549.
Blaeu's Atlas, Amsterdam, 1654. Surveyed by Timothy Pont about 1608.
A Tour through the whole Island of Great Britain, Defoe, 1742.
A Tour of Scotland, 1769, Thos. Pennant.
View of the Mineralogy, Agriculture, Manufactures and Fisheries of the Island of Arran, Rev. James Headrick (1807).
The Highlands and Western Isles of Scotland, John Macculloch, M.D. (1924).
The Geology of the Island of Arran from Original Survey, A. C. Ramsay (1841).
Arran: a Poem in Six Cantos, Rev. David Landsborough (1847).
Excursion to Arran, Ailsa Craig, etc., Rev. David Landsborough.
Guide to the Highlands and Islands, Anderson (1850).
Circuit Journeys, Lord Cockburn (1842). Published 1889.
The Geology of Arran, etc., James Bryce, M.A. 1872.
Days at the Coast, Hugh Macdonald (1857).
The Geology of North Arran, South Bute, and the Cumbraes, with parts of Ayrshire and Kintyre, W. Gunn, Sir Archd. Geikie, B. N. Peach and A. Harker (1903).
The British Highlands with Rope and Rucksack, E. A. Baker.
Arran of the Bens, the Glens, and the Brave, Mackenzie MacBride, F.S.A., and J. Lawton Wingate, R.S.A.
The Book of Arran, Hugh Hopkins, 1910 and 1914.
All about Arran, R. Angus Downie.
Tramping in Arran, Tom S. Hall.
Bute and the Cumbraes, R. Angus Downie.
The Geology of Arran, G. W. Tyrrell (1928).
Mountaineering in Scotland and Undiscovered Scotland, W. H. Murray.
Rock Climbs in Arran, W. M. M. Wallace (1970).

In the *Scottish Mountaineering Club Journal* –
    Vol. 1, p. 31, 'The Glen Sannox Hills' by T. Fraser and S. Campbell.
          2, p. 17, 'Cir Mhor from Glen Sannox' by W. W. Naismith.
          3, p.195, 'The Granite Peaks of Arran' by W. Douglas.
          3, p.212, 'Cir Mhor' by Gilbert Thomson.
          5, p. 29, 'A Day on Cir Mhor' by W. Inglis Clark.

7, p. 1, 'Ben Nuis Chimney' by L. J. Oppenheimer.

8, p. 12, 'Arran' by F. S. Goggs.

23, p.180, 'New Climbs in Arran' by G. C. Curtis and G. Townend.

23, p.236, 'Arran 1944' by G. C. Curtis and G. Townend.

23, p.415, 'Golden Eagles in Arran' by G. C. Curtis and G. Townend.

22, p.320, 'South Ridge, Rosa Pinnacle, Cir Mhor' by J. F. Hamilton.

23, p. 45, 'Ben Tarsuinn, No. 2 Chimney'.

24, p.237, 'Goatfell and Am Binnein' by E. Rudge.

NEW CLIMBS:

Vol. 26, pp. 66, 306, 387.

27, pp. 269, 364.

28, pp. 34, 111, 126, 212, 227, 318, 340.

29, pp. 56, 77, 185, 201, 284.

In the *Rucksack Club Journal*, Vol. 10, No. 4, p. 228 (1946–7) 'The re-Discovery of Arran' by J. R. Jenkins.

2
The Clyde to Ardnamurchan

BUTE

Windy Hill (911 ft.) Approximately 1 mile north of—
Kames Hill (875 ft.) 2 miles north-west of Port Bannatyne.
Barone Hill (530 ft.) 2 miles south-west of Rothesay.
Maps: One-inch O.S., Seventh Series, Sheet 71.
      Half-inch Bartholomew, sheet 44.

ACCESS:
Steamers from Wemyss Bay to Rothesay, approximately every two hours throughout the day. A ferry operates from Colintraive on the mainland to Rhubodach. Bus services operate which give access to all parts of the island.

Though the Highland Fault Line cuts through Bute, the island is Lowland country. The highest point on the island is in the north where Windy Hill rises to 911 ft. The climber may prefer Kames Hill: though lower it is a better point from which to view wistfully the peaks of Arran.

Being mostly fertile arable land, Bute has none of the shell sand, marram grass and flower bedecked machair of the Hebrides.

KAMES HILL and WINDY HILL are reached by either taking a bus or walking from Rothesay to Port Bannatyne, then around Kames Bay to a lane leading up to two hillside farms. After passing the farms, one comes to more open hillside above the trees. The approach to Windy Hill from Kames Hill is over ridges and marshy dips, where there is some bog cotton. The heather on the upper slopes is rigorously burnt.

The road between Ettrick Bay and Rhubodach makes a pleasant walk. If one wants to be more adventurous, one may follow the coast. One would want to clear out of Ettrick Bay – though the tramcars no longer run there. The road is relatively quiet, narrow and wild and passes through matured woods of oak and birch. BARLIA HILL

(321 ft.) on the right has a shapely ridge. Near Kilmichael there is a small chapel, hardly worth visiting except for the view down the Kyles.

In the south, a little over a mile south-west of Kilchattan Bay are the remains of St. Blane's Chapel, a Norman church of the twelfth century. A circular structure near the church, probably goes back to the time of St. Blane, who died in 590. Just to the west near the shore is the vitrified fort of Dunagoil. St. Blane's Seat (399 ft.) is a good viewpoint about half a mile from Garroch Head. The bay which looks across at the Cock of Arran, though only a couple of hundred yards from the road, is secluded and unspoilt, with clean sands.

For leaflets and information about nature trails, rights-of-way and paths, and plants, birds and other wild life, apply to the Museum, Rothesay.

GREAT CUMBRAE

Gaid Stone, Barbay Hill (417 ft.) Centre of island.
Horse Hill (255 ft.) Half a mile west of Dwoncraig ferry.
Aird Hill (161 ft.) in north-east.
Aird Hill (159 ft.) in south-west.

Maps: One-inch O.S., Seventh Series, sheet 66.
Half-inch, Bartholomew, sheet 44.

ACCESS:
Frequent steamer service from Wemyss Bay, Largs and Fairlie to Keppel and Millport Old Piers. A good flat road follows closely around the coast. Bicycles may be hired in Millport.

The hill behind Millport – a cathedral city – has rock outcrops. The Diel's Dyke and Lion Rock near Keppel Pier are basaltic dykes. The main Marine Laboratory for the Clyde (museum) is in Millport.

LITTLE CUMBRAE

Summit (406 ft.)

ACCESS:
From Millport, Great Cumbrae by hiring boat.

The island is separated from the Great Cumbrae by the half-mile wide Tan Sound.

On top of the highest point is an ancient lighthouse tower on which a fire of coals, or 'cresset' was kept burning in an open grate. The present lighthouse is on the west shore of the island. There are rock outcrops at the southern end. The square keep on Castle Island on the east shore, inside Trail Island is twin of one on the mainland at Portencross. The remains of the chapel of St. Vey lie a short distance north.

AILSA CRAIG

Summit (1114 ft.).
Maps: One-inch O.S., Seventh Series, sheet 72
    Half-inch Bartholomew, sheet 40.

ACCESS:
Ferry by arrangement from Girvan.

The route to the summit is directly from the landing place on the east shore. The crossing from the mainland, though only 10 miles and taking just over the hour in a fishing-boat, is exposed, as there are no sheltering islands west of Ailsa Craig. It is advisable to take provisions for an extra day's stay. There is no difficulty in the ascent, but in places one has to climb over steeply inclined, slabby boulders. On all the other aspects of the cone but the east, are tremendous cliffs.

Reibickite, a micro-granite, is one of the constitute rocks, and the Red Stone Quarry was the source of red-coloured curling stones. Much of the island is composed of columnal basalt, sometimes forming columns of around 400 ft. in height. Bare Stack is a stupendous cliff situated in the north-west which sweeps upwards in two ferocious brown overhangs of some 500 ft., too inhospitable even for gannets to nest.

Ashydoo cliff lies just south, and on the south-west corner is Water Cave; reminiscent of Fingal's Cave on Staffa on a smaller scale. An exposed corner has to be negotiated in order to reach the cave from the eastward around the shore, past Little Ailsa.

If one likes birds the spring is the best time to visit Ailsa Craig. It is one of the main breeding grounds of the gannet. Puffins, guillemots, kittiwakes and gulls are amongst the sea-birds to be found. Of the land birds the domestic blackbirds, song-thrush, wheatears and willow warbler have been seen. Pipits may be found on the steep slopes above the smooth rock walls.

At the same time the flowers are varied and delightful. The higher slopes are a field of wild hyacinths, rising from the sea to the heights. In crevices of the granite, the thrift contrasts with fresh green of young grass. In places the cliffs are white with the scented flowers of scurvy grass, and here and there flowers of the red lychnis are to be seen swaying in the breeze.

The ruins of an old castle are set precariously on these slopes. Three stars – the Hamilton coat of arms – have been carved on a stone set in the walls.

Ailsa Craig is sometimes known as Creag Ealasaid – Elizabeth's Rock. In the old Irish tale of Buioe Suibne it is called Carraig Alastair (Irish Text Society).

DAVAAR

Summit (378 ft.).

Maps: One-inch O.S., Seventh Series, sheet 65.
Half-inch Bartholomew, sheet 43.

ACCESS:

Lying at the entrance to Campbeltown Loch it is only an island when the tide is more than half full. At low water it is joined to the mainland by a spit of gravel over half a mile long called the Dhorlin.

The summit (trig. point) is a good viewpoint over the widest stretch of the Firth of Clyde to the north. A traverse round the shore is an enjoyable expedition. The sea birds are plentiful. As well as the many varieties of wader to be seen around the Dhorlin, at the south-east corner, duck – mostly eider – are numerous, and gannets in fair numbers are to be seen as dazzling white flashes in the sunlight.

200 yards east of the cave containing the famous painting is a rock rib – steep and strenuous at the start – which gives an interesting line to the top. Further round to the east, when in sight of the light-house, a grassy rake gives easy access to the summit through, in May, solid masses of giant violets and wild hyacinth.

The painting, though modern – it was done in 1887 by Alexander MacKinnon, and retouched by the artist himself again in 1934 – is interesting. It is life-size and is on the back wall of an alcove, where the form and contour of the rock face has been used to give another dimension to the figure; which is that of the crucified Christ. The colours are not over garish blue and white, and the work is competent, especially the face and eyes. To the right is the face of a cherub.

The walk to the caves takes a very leisurely two hours. The summit of the island is heather clad, in contrast to the rather uninteresting arable land elsewhere round Campbeltown, and wild primeval-looking St. Kildan sheep hold the heights.

SANDA

Summit (405 ft.).
Maps: One-inch O.S., Seventh Series, sheet 65.
Half-inch Bartholomew, sheet 43.

ACCESS:
Boat by arrangement from Southend. The island lies 1½ miles from Southend at the southernmost tip of the Mull of Kintyre. It contains a ruined chapel with the reputed grave of St. Ninian. Anyone who walked over the spot was supposed to die within the year.

Directly to the south of the landing place is an outcrop with a deep gully up the centre, which might be worth investigating.

Hires may be arranged with A. Cameron, Dunaverty, Southend. Tel. 239.

CARA

Summit 185 ft. at the Mull of Cara.
Maps: One-inch O.S., Seventh Series, sheet 65.
Half-inch Bartholomew, sheet 43.

ACCESS:
Boat by arrangement from Kilmory.
There is a ruined chapel on the island.

In 1615 Sir James Macdonald of Islay based his fleet there when he rebelled against royal authority. He was defeated by Argyll's forces which mustered at Duntroon Castle.

GIGHA

Creag Bhan (331 ft.)

Maps: One-inch O.S., Seventh Series, sheet 58.
    Half-inch Bartholomew, sheet 43.

ACCESS:
By MacBraynes from West Loch Tarbert. Passenger ferry between Tayinloan and Ardminish, operated by MacKechnie, Tel. Gigha 217. Crossing time 20 minutes. Car hire – McSporran, Post Office. Tel. Gigha 211.

ACCOMMODATION:
Accommodation may be found on the spot, but during the season, one would be well advised to be prepared to camp. Hotel at Ardminish.

It is a gentle walk to the highest point of the island, where the ice-scored slabs are amongst the best examples of glaciated rock in Scotland, and the view of Jura is superb on a fine day. The very top of Creag Bhan geologists say was the only part of the island to keep its head above the ice-field during the Ice Age. The main physical feature of the island is a long spinal ridge of epidiorite forming hummocky hills and falling to a narrow strip of coastal plain. In the north and west they are bold like some of the less riven parts of the Cuillin; the rock clean. Deep glens either side carry brawling streams to the sea. On the west is a rugged coast of small cliffs.

The Raven's Rock at the north end is so named because of a local belief that Noah had a raven, not a dove, which landed there.

There are many caves along the coast, some on old raised beaches, some still at sea-level.

On the island are the ruins of the ancient church of Kilchattan, the 'Oghan Stone' and a Norse Thing Mound – the only one in the Hebrides.

The plant collection in the garden of Achamore House belonging to Sir James Horlick may be viewed throughout the summer. It includes many valuable specimens.

DANNA

Mid Danna (178 ft.)
Maps: One-inch O.S., Seventh Series, sheet 58.
Half-inch Bartholomew, 43.

ACCESS:
Reached by a stone causeway from the peninsula to the north, it lies at the mouth of Loch Sween. It is fringed by rocky islands, the furthest out is –

EILEAN MHOR which is an island of no great height, and shaped like a green anthill. It is, however, one of Scotland's most ancient holy places. Half a mile long and uninhabited. A boat from Crinan Hotel may be hired for visiting the island.

A twelfth-century chapel with a nave and vaulted chancel is dedicated to St. Carmaig. The saint's original cell, built five hundred years earlier (he died in 664) is near the south end. On the island's highest point, near the cell, is a Celtic cross-shaft. North of the church are traces of a beehive cell and other buildings unknown.

KINTYRE was created an island after the treaty of 1095 when Malcolm III acknowledged the right of Magnus Barefoot, or rather Barelegs (as King of the Isles he adopted the native dress) to those islands, between which, and the mainland a ship could pass. Barelegs had himself hauled in his galley from the East to the West Loch.

THE FAIRY ISLES at the head of Loch Sween are a bird sanctuary. Duck and swan are mostly to be found. They lie in an inlet between Caol and Scotnish, the main loch. They may be reached by boat from Tayviallich, 2 miles. There is a strong current on the ebb from the Caol Scotnish. There are seven principal islands, mostly wooded and clad with heathers. The area can be reached by walking by Loch Coille Bharr, 3 miles down the peninsula, and entering the forest $4\frac{1}{2}$ miles north of Tayviallich at a right angled bend near the loch. The forestry tract – no vehicles allowed – leads down to the shore opposite the Fairy Isles.

7. Kerrera, Gylan Castle.

8. Islay, coast near Port Ellan.

ISLAY

Sgarbh Breac (1192 ft.)
Beinn Bheigeir (1609 ft.)
Beinn Bhan (1544 ft.)
Maps: One-inch O.S., Seventh Series, sheet 57.
Half-inch Bartholomew, sheet 43.

ACCESS:

From West Loch Tarbert, calling at Port Ellen, Port Askaig. Mac-Braynes run two boats daily; one only Sunday. Western Ferries run from Kennacraig; three boats either way every day; two on Sundays, at cheaper rates than MacBraynes (to Port Askaig only). A ferry is run from Port Askaig to Feolin on Jura in association with Western Ferries, by arrangement with Mr. McPhie, Port Askaig.

Two planes daily – summer service – from Abbotsinch to Islay, via Campbeltown. The afternoon plane from Islay does not call at Campbeltown.

Bus service from Port Askaig, Bowmore, Portnahaven, also Bowmore, Kilchoman Circle and Port Charlotte, Bowmore, Glenegedale Airport.

CENTRES AND ACCOMMODATION:

The best centres are Port Ellen (hotels) near the south end, Bowmore (hotels) near the head of Loch Indaal, and Port Askaig (hotel) on the Sound of Islay opposite Jura. Bowmore is most central. Bicycles can be hired here.

Beinn Bheigeir (1609 ft.), the highest hill on the island, is of quartzite rock.

Possibly the most interesting line of ascent is from the south-east by following the Claggain river to the edge of the tree line, then up steep ground to gain the end of the south-east ridge (map reference 443553).

Glas Bheinn (1455 ft.) and the nearby **Beinn Bhan** (1544 ft.) are probably best approached from the south up Glen Phroaig from the east coast, up the true right bank of the stream.

The eastern region of the island is rolling wild upland stretching from the hill-and-loch area north-east of Port Ellen to the extremity of the island at Rudha A'Mhail.

The southernmost tip, the Mull of Oa is the farthest south cape of the Hebrides – as some say 'within easy reach of the North Irish coast'. It looks straight to the Antrim hills in the original Scottish kingdom of Dalriada. The rare and elusive chough breeds in this region – one of the few places it can be found in Scotland. There is a very bad road to a croft at Upper Killeyan. From there it is a half mile walk to the Mull. The cliffs here are highly recommended to 'scramblers'. At the farm of Sannaig Mor there are 600 ft. high cliffs.

A superb arête of clean granite drops from the Cairn of Beinn Mhor, near the Mull of Oa, straight to sea level. It gives at least 500 ft. of climbing, probably free for most of its height; the bottom hundred feet seems to fall vertically to the waves, and artificial methods may be needed here. East of this are at least two other good steep granite ridges, of some 300 ft. length. The whole area of coast east of the American Monument offers scope for good new routes.

Also, on the north-west coast at the Rhinns, there are fine cliffs. If northward bound, beyond Rudha Bhachlaig one keeps above the broken ground, a mile and a half's walking takes one to the raised beaches, which here are high, flat-topped and pebbly. Islay's north and Jura's west coast raised beaches are world famous.

Sgarbh Breac (1192 ft.) is the highest hill in northern Islay, and is best reached by way of the summit of **Beinn Thrasda** (852 ft.) (map reference 412778) from which it is separated by a col.

Kildalton, the area at the south-eastern corner of the island has a castle, a finely proportioned chapel (map reference 458509) and a graveyard containing the Kildalton Cross, the principal art treasure of Islay.

JURA

Beinn Shaintaidh (1930 ft.)
Corra Bheinn (1867 ft.)
Beinn An Oir (2571 ft.)
Beinn A Chaolais (2407 ft.)
Maps: One-inch O.S., Seventh Series, sheets 51 and 57.
      Half-inch Bartholomew, sheet 43.

ACCESS:
Ferry (MacBraynes) from West Loch Tarbert to Craighouse (same service as for Port Askaig, Islay). Western Ferries from Kennacraig,

West Loch Tarbert to Port Askaig, Islay, then McPhie's ferry to Feoline.

A road runs from Feoline up the east coast past Craighouse and Tarbert to Ardlussa. The route from Feoline directly towards the hills, though boggy at first, becomes drier as one goes inland.

A passenger ferry runs from Carsaig, Tayvallich, to Ardlussa, weather and other circumstances permitting. Arrangements may be made with B. S. Moore, Farm House, Ardlussa. Tel. Jura 24.

A bus, which runs in connection with the MacBraynes ferry only, connects Craighouse with Inverlussa, via Lagg. There is a car hire service between Feoline and Craighouse.

Beinn Shaintaidh (2477 ft., the Consecrated Hill) is the easternmost of the Paps and is most easily reached by turning north where the road goes over the Corran River (map reference 544721), keeping to the true right bank up under a conspicuous rectangular coniferous plantation. Thus one leaves the river and boggy land to the right, and gains altitude relatively easily to Loch an t-Stob. Cross the river where it leaves the loch (map reference 523736). A steep slope of 1930 ft. of fine quartzite scree, heather and moss leads to the summit.

Corra Bheinn which might be termed the fourth Pap, lies to the north-east of Shaintaidh. The route drops to the complicated series of lochans on the pass between. The ascent and descent of this lesser peak is steep, but only 650 ft. and adds about 3 miles to the total.

Beinn An Oir (the Boundary Hill) is reached by following the west ridge from Beinn Shaintaidh down the 1450 ft. col. This western slope is the only one not steep enough to be a scree slope – just where it would be welcome to run down. The ridge up to the summit has a causeway erected on it by the Ordnance Survey over a century ago. In 1812 experiments were made here to determine the various temperatures at which water boils according to altitude.

Beinn A Chaolais (the Hill of Kyle) is the south-westernmost and lowest of the trio of fine hills known as the Paps. To reach it from Beinn an Oir triangulation station descend the south spur, avoiding the steep ground on the right overlooking Na Garbh-lochanan corrie, to the col at 1214 ft. (map reference 496741). It is less than a mile, but up a scree slope again from the col to the summit.

The descent can be made either to Feoline and the ferry to Islay, or to Keils by a lochan dotted shoulder which sweeps down above the head of Glen Astaile. Cut across the head streams of Abhainn Mhic'ill Libhri, and under the eastern slopes of Glas Beinn and down to the stream which passes the Earnadail graveyard (map reference 524688). Keep to the northern bank and from the graveyard take the untarred track for a short distance, turning right to the crofting settlement of Keils, less than a mile from Craighouse.

From Feoline, by skirting round the west side of Beinn a'Chaolais, one reaches the north-west ridge of Beinn an Oir, which is here an easy slope of grass and stones, below the scree angle, leading to a dip in the summit ridge a little north of the cairn. The side of Beinn Shaintaidh facing is the only one again not steep enough to be scree covered.

Though Islay is the largest of this small group of islands Jura overshadows it. The Paps are not far short of the hills of Arran; the highest Pap at 2571 ft. is only a little lower than Goat Fell.

Travelling is difficult on the island. It has only one small section of road round the south end. Yet the mountains of Jura are almost as famous as those of Skye, and have drawn the attention of artists such as MacTaggart and his contemporaries and followers.

Besides being one of the wildest of all Scottish islands, Jura is now one of the least populated in proportion to former times. There can be no wilder upland region in Britian, and in the Hebrides the only islands to compare with it are Rum and Harris. The geology and topography are mainly responsible for the lack of development; but also the fact that Jura like Rum and Harris, has long been kept as a sporting estate.

Most of the island is deer forest. In the west there is not a single habitation. The Norsemen named Jura 'Diera' which means deer island. Another possible derivation of the name is Dura or Doura from dull or dour.

Am Fraoch Eilean and Borsdale Island lie off the south coast.

There is no other coast so rich in caves and arches as the western shore, nor so many raised beaches over long stretches. The land at Jura's northern end, and Scarba's southern is relatively high and slopes steeply down to the shores of the Gulf of Corrievrecken. To reach Corrievrecken one must go northwards along the road beyond Ardlussa, past Lealt and Barnhill to the remote shepherd's cottage of Kinuachdrach. From here it is fully three miles over rough ground to the northern end of the gulf.

It ranges in depth from 300 to 900 ft. and the constriction of water is made all the worse by great overfalls and numerous whirlpools. The most formidable feature is the Great Whirlpool which forms close under the Scarba shore at Bagh Ban, said to be the second largest whirlpool in the world. It is known to Hebrideans as 'The Hag'. Andrew Arthur of Soay has passed through it on the Jura side several times. He said that the island of Eilean Mhor looked particularly impressive from the gulf. Campbell Steven said that when the tide was on the ebb the currents in the middle of the gulf were playing strange tricks. The general impression was one of immense latent power, though the only obvious unruliness occurred opposite the place of the main whirlpool, where a line of surf kept creaming along the black rocks of Scarba with its three conical and conspicuous hills which seem to attract to themselves more clouds than any other mountains of the west.

The only safe period for negotiation of the gulf, even for a large vessel, is said to be at a quarter of an hour around slack water. John Dunn (S.M.C.) has canoed through it and lived to tell the tale. It is one of the great spectacles of the Scottish scene, comparable in impressiveness to the great cliff of Conachair in St. Kilda.

The name is properly Coire Breachain. Breacan was either a Norwegian prince or an Irish merchant, whose ships were engulfed. He was buried in a cave nearby on the south side of the bay, Bagh nam Muc, which cuts deeply into the land just west of the northern-most point of the island. Martin Martin stated in 1695 that the cave had Breacan's stone, a tomb and an altar in it.

It seems pertinent here to mention the Dhourus Mor (the Great Door) directly opposite Corrievrecken to the east; the narrow gap between Craignish Point on the mainland and the islet of Garbh Reis. An important passage for vessels western bound through the barrier, it is three cables long and three across between Craignish Point and Garraesar, a small barren islet to the south. The tides sluices through this gut at 8 knots springs. There is a side door; an eddy round Craignish Point, with the help of which, and a bit of luck, the flood may be cheated. Try it on a quiet day.

SCARBA

Cruach Scarba (1478 ft.)

Maps: One-inch O.S., Seventh Series, sheet 52.
　　　Half-inch Bartholomew, sheet 44.
　　　Admiralty Chart, 2326.

ACCESS:

A boat may be hired at Black Mill Bay, Luing. The ferryman works the Gulf of Corrievrecken lobster fishing.

Kilmory Lodge is the only inhabited house. The climb to the highest point from Kilmory has no difficulty. There is a low spine of rock at the top. It is an excellent point from which to view the Garvallochs and Corrievrecken. Though the western flank falls steeply to the shore rocks, it consists of heather with occasional steeper walls of unstable blocks plastered liberally with vegetation.

A signal fire is the only method of emergency communication, so be warned not to light fires indiscriminately – it may bring a doctor or a full-scale rescue party.

SEIL

Meall a'Chaise (479 ft.)

Maps: O.S. one-inch, Seventh Series, sheet 52.
　　　Half-inch Bartholomew, sheet 44.

ACCESS:

—over the 'bridge over the Atlantic' from Clachan on the mainland. Seil is a splendid viewpoint for the Garvelloch islands and the magnificent, rugged south coast of Mull. From Easdale northwards there is a pleasant scramble round the base of the cliffs which are loose higher up. There is an impasse after half a mile which might yield to artificial tactics up a crack in the face. Near the summit of Meall a'Chaise are the remains of a strong fort, Lossgann Lornach, built to resist the Vikings.

From Seil there is a ferry to Luing, which however only plies for a short time each day owing to the fierce tides between the islands.

The north-west ridge of Luing, which is entirely of slate – much quarried – gives a precarious climb. One would be better browsing amongst the sea pinks, scabious, orchids, and Scots lovage which grows profusely.

When approaching the Easdale village (Ellanbeich) the escarpment will be seen above the road. It is an outlying area of the Lower Old Red Standstone, which occupies the north-west part of Seil, on which it is pleasanter to scramble.

Quarrying operations on the island ceased abruptly when the sea rushed in and filled the deep pit of the quarry in the same great storm of 1879 that destroyed the first Tay Bridge.

KERRERA

Carn Breugach (617 ft.)

ACCESS:
Ferry from Oban, or a shorter crossing from a point two miles south along the Gallanach road.

A good place to visit from Oban on a wet day of bad weather when one hasn't the heart or the stomach for the longer crossing to Mull, is Gylen Castle, which has an interesting passage underneath and can look formidable on a grim day. On the way one passes the lobster pools, which may hold as many as a thousand occupants, awaiting shipment to the market from Cullipool.

GARVELLOCH ISLES (Isles of the Sea).

Garbh Eilach (362 ft.)
Maps: One-inch O.S., Seventh Series, sheet 51.
      Half-inch Bartholomew, sheet 47.

ACCESS:
Boat hire from MacAllister, The Moorings, Cuan Ferry, or D. McCorquodale, The Ferry, Easdale, Tel. Balvicar 200x, or Black Mill Bay, Luing.

The Garvellochs lie in the middle of the Firth of Lorne half-way between Scarba and Mull. There is a good sheltered landing place with jetty at an inlet on Garbh Eilach where the north-eastern escarpment gives way to green slopes.

From north-east to south-west the islands are Dun Chonnuill, Garbh Eilach, A'Chuli, Sgeir Leth a'Chuain and Eilach na Naoimh.

M. Slesser and J. S. Stewart investigated a deep cleft near the centre of the Garbh Eilach face and did some routes on the side walls, reporting limestone cliffs with Dolomite-like routes, but hardly on Dolomite scale. The worthy Dr. Macculloch perhaps hyperbolises when he writes that: '— there are none of the Western Islands which can compete with these for beauty in so small a space. Calypso herself might have exchanged her domains for the Garveloch. The view from the summit is various, magnificent, and extensive; the height appearing to be about 700 ft.'

The actual (362 ft.) summit of Garbh Eilach is difficult to find, the map shows it near the eastern end of the backbone ridge, but careful searching failed to reveal a cairn. The northern cliffs are so steep it is quite easy to throw a stone from their tops into the surf.

The islands consist of two members of the Dalriadan sequence, a white or pale limestone and a group which may be named collectively the Boulder Beds, largely of quartzite. These rocks have been thrown into a succession of sharp folds – the white limestone in the cores of the folds.

On Eileach na Naiomh (252 ft.) – the Isle of the Saints – there is the monastery of Ailech founded by St. Brendan about 542. The remains of the buildings, which, since the island has been long uninhabited are in remarkably good shape, are probably the oldest of their kind in Scotland. Apart from the monastery, there are two beehive cells (one of which has been restored by the Ministry of Works and now stands more than 10 ft. high), an underground cell and an oratory.

COLONSAY

Beinn Bhreac (401 ft.)
Car nan Eoin (470 ft.)
Beinn Breac (another) (450 ft.)
Bei na Coarach (412 ft.)
Beinn nan Gudairean (445 ft.)
Carn Mor (438 ft.)

Maps: One-inch O.S. Seventh Series, sheet 51.
Half-inch Bartholomew, sheet 43.

9. Jura, from Eilean Mor.

10. Corrievrecken and Jura.

11. Colonsay, Kiloran Bay.

ACCESS:

MacBraynes ferry from West Loch Tarbert, Kintyre.

ACCOMMODATION:

Hotel at Scalascaig.

Good campsites at Port Mor and Port Lubh, though they are apt to be taken by school holiday camps during school holidays. There are numerous other good sites in the west – Kiloran is accessible and has water. High winds are prevalent. Tents of conventional design tend to be blown down, and the launching of canoes or small boats is often impracticable.

CLIMBING:

Bheinn Bhreac gives some amusing scrambling on the west side, southern end. An escarpment runs northward, mostly vegetatious and overhanging, culminating in an overhang 200 ft. high: a miniature Sgurr Scaladale. There is white limestone at the northern end.

If the north-west corner is taken directly, the starting move is somewhat awkward. Easy to moderate routes will be found on the south-west corner of Carn nan Eoin immediately north of Kiloran Bay.

Beinn Breac, the highest summit on the island at 456 ft., lies between Port Mor and Kiloran. It has a steep west face, like a jutting prow, and in general form resembles the inverted flowerpot shape of a Sutherland peak.

At Port Mor, just up from the Dun Meadonach, there is a grass defile, clearly seen from the road. It has a small overhang on the right, and a short but useful practice slab on the left.

Beinn na Caorach's south-west ridge gives fully 300 ft. on good easy rock (Torridorian sandstone): from sea-level to the top of a splendid miniature mountain. The west face which is wet, loose and vegetatious and at least vertical, might provide some highly artificial amusement.

All the climbing may be graded as suitable for 10-to-15-year-olds.

At the north-west corner of the island, near Leac Bluide, there are the remains of a chapel, a standing stone and a cross. Many of the relics and remains on the island are early Christian – pre Columban. The abbey at Kiloran was called after St. Oran.

In the central part of the island, which is not so interesting as the coast, there is much sea beach debris, since Colonsay was originally four smaller islands.

The old burial ground is at Balaruminmore in the south-east. It is a fine point to view the Paps of Jura, especially in the evening. A cross and a carved slab, much worn, are to be found there.

At Garvard, adjoining Oronsay, there are the foundations of a cell or chapel, a dun, and a standing stone around which field gentians may be found blooming in late summer.

ORONSAY

Beinn Oronsay (304 ft.)

Maps: One-inch O.S., Seventh Series, sheet 51.
Half-inch Bartholomew, sheet 43.

ACCESS:
From Colonsay by the Strand at Garvard, when it should be possible for two hours either side of low water – 5 ft. at deepest place at high water.

There is an outcrop of rock above the priory on the south side of Beinn Oronsay.

The ruins of the Priory of Oronsay are next in interest to those of Iona – amongst the finest of Ecclesiastical antiquities. Near the church is a very beautiful 12 ft. high cross. Another cross on a 3 ft. stem stands on a plinth at the east end. The collection of carved stones, which is housed nearby, is superb.

REFERENCES:

Sculptured Stones of Islay, Graham.
Popular Tales of the West Highlands, John F. Campbell.
Frost and Fire (a remarkable geological work), J. F. Cam.
The House of Islay, Domhnull Gruamach. (A short history of Somerled and the Lords of the Isles.)
The Foundations of Islay, Domhnull Gruamach. (Graham Donald. A valuable commentary on Celtic history.)
The New Naturalist, Vol. 1 (Collins) – article on the birds of Ailsa Craig.

Argyll's Highlands, C. Bede (pub., J. MacKay), 1902.
The Island Hills, Campbell Stephen (Hurst & Blackett).
Jura, Donald Budge (pub. J. Smith, Glasgow).
The Book of Coll and Tiree, Erskine Beveridge, 1903.
Colonsay and Oronsay, J. de V. Loder, 1935.
The Book of Colonsay and Oronsay, Symington Grieve, 1923.
The West Coast Pilot.
The *Scottish Mountaineering Club Journal* –
    Vol. 3, p. 164, 'Jura' by H. B. Watt.
        19, p. 281, 'Jura' by J. Rooke Corbett.

3
Mull and adjacent islands

LISMORE

Barr Mor Summit 417 ft. and south end near Achadun.

Maps: One-inch O.S., Seventh Series, sheet 46.
Half-inch Bartholomew, sheet 47.

ACCESS:

Passenger ferry several times daily from Port Appin; steamer and boat hire from Oban. Car hire – J. Stewart, The Mill, Lismore. Tel. 221. Boat hire to North Isles of Lismore and Castle Stalker, contact S. MacDonald, 2 Station Cottages, Appin.

A road runs the ten-mile length of Lismore.

If the highest point is climbed the view is dominated by Duart Point and Castle and the Hills of Mull to the west. The view northeast up Loch Linnhe to the great mountains of Glencoe and Nevis is particularly fine in winter conditions.

M. Slesser, D. Small and N. Tennent have done some very severe top-rope routes on the south-east cliffs. The landmark to the routes is a conspicuous cave opposite to the north end of Eilean na Cloich. The face around the cave is in the region of 80 ft. high. Elsewhere on the escarpment – which is a raised beach – the height is somewhat less.

Eilean na Cloiche (Island of the Stone), a boldly-shaped rock rising almost straight out of the sea for 60 to 80 ft., offers a route starting in the centre of a slab of rock. Then up a crack to the left of an outcrop for 20 ft. At the top of this ledge traverse right and finish up a perpendicular wall to the top. The top 5 ft. is loose rock and grass. Done by Allan Arthur in 1917.

Eilean Dubh off the middle-east coast of Lismore is worth a visit by canoe, but not to do the south face of the north top which is 50 ft.

of very loose, vegetatious (barbed and prickly) and overhanging rubble.

Lismore – the name means the great garden – is a mass of limestone, very green and fertile. Field gentians, the common centuary – surely one of the most delightful of our native gentians – eyebright, rock rose (helianthemum) mimulus, tutsan, cranesbill, ivy-leaved toadflax, and water mints, brooklimes and speedwells in profusion, are to be found.

A fine broch, Tirefour Castle, is near the village of Clachan, opposite Eilean Dubh. There is a cave believed to have been inhabited by St. Kieran when he evangelised Lismore.

MULL – A headland.

Eastern Group:	**Maol Buidhe** (1201 ft.): **Beinn Chreagach Mhor** (1903 ft.): **Beinn Mheadon** (2087 ft.): **Dun da Ghaoithe** (2512 ft.)
Central Group:	(Divided from the latter by Glen Forsa): **Ben Talaidh** (2496 ft.): **Cruach Choreadail** (2026 ft.): **Corra Beinn** (2309 ft.): **Cruachan Dearg** (2309 ft.)
Southern Group:	(Divided from the latter by Glen More). **Creach Beinn** (2289 ft.): **Beinn Buie** (2354 ft. and 2341 ft.)
Western Group:	(Divided from Central Group by Glen Chachaig). **Beinn Fhada** (2304 ft.): **Ben More** (3169 ft.)
Maps:	One-inch O.S., Seventh Series, sheets 45, 51 and 52. Half-inch Bartholomew, sheet 47.

ACCESS:

The island of Mull lies off the west coast of Argyll, 20 minutes sailing from Morven and Ardnamurchan on the mainland, and by the regular service to Craignure from Oban.

Frequent car ferry service (summer – four sailings per day – 45 minutes), from Oban and Craignure, whence bus connections to Tobermory and Fionnphort for Iona. Steamer from Fort William to Tobermory via Oban daily.

The three main daily bus services run in conjunction with the steamer services from Tobermory and Craignure. In winter time the buses only pay their way by virtue of the mail contract, and passengers must follow the mail routes.

Most visitors to the island disembark at Craignure when coming from the south via Oban, and bus services which run southabout through the Lussa valley (Glenmore) to Loch Scridain and the Iona ferry, or northabout via Salen, give very convenient access to most of the hills.

Mull – General

Measuring 25 miles from north to south and from 3 miles at the Salen – Loch na Keal neck to 20 miles at its widest, Mull is the biggest of the Inner Hebrides after Skye. There is more variety of scenery than on the other mountainous islands, and the scene changes quickly as the roads are narrow, twisty and hilly.

The main body of the island is mountainous, rising to 3169 ft. at Ben More. Its head is gentler country of wide moors divided by the long shallow valley of Glen Aros. The leg of the Ross is wild, treeless and bare, with a few arboreal pockets at the west end. The climate is mild and the rainfall fairly high at 80 to 90 inches – it is said to be similar to Cornwall in rainfall and temperature. The north and south-west are slightly drier and windier, being farther from the big hills.

As with many islands the charm of Mull is a matter of intimacy. One gets the cold shoulder off the north coast, where the little cliffs are uninspiring and the hills lacking in grandeur. After canoeing round the south coast Robin Chalmers said it was better than East Greenland, which is praise indeed.

Mull excels Rhum and most of its other neighbours in the beauty of its mountain forms. Take Ben More from the west, Beinn Talaidh from the north – surely one of the most shapely hills in Scotland – or Ben Buie from Creach Beinn, with the glorious interplay of light over the rolling moorland like the westward seas; or the south coast with its awesome cliffs soaring to a climax at Malcolm's Point and the great mountains behind, from seaward, or Seil Island, or Easdale – as exciting as the Cuillin from Elgol.

In the corries of Ben More is fine grazing so that the stags there are of exceptionally heavy weight. Ptarmigan nest on the slopes of Ben Buie, though only 2200 ft., for on the Atlantic seaboard seemingly, the birds frequent hills which in the Central Highlands would be too low for their requirements.

The north-west of the island though itself less dramatic, commands a seascape as magnificently rich in features as any in the west coast.

Bays everywhere around the coast are varied and interesting. The Ross of Mull is low-lying primeval moorland, such as one finds in the outer isles and the far north. There are few inland lochs – only ten of any size despite the rainfall – due to the relatively good drainage. There is little heather. The underlying rock is tertiary basalt in the mountain areas, which weathers into terraces. The butt of the Ross is granite but the largest mass of the mountains is gabbro, which where it extrudes, does so in the form of screes, or at best in relatively small outcrops and crags.

There is a reasonable driving road from Loch Spelve on the Firth of Lorne westward to Loch Scridain through Glen More, a distance of about 10 miles. The glen once was the boundary between the Picts and the Scots. Though the glen as a whole is bare and arid, it is wooded in the vicinity of Loch Spelve. Interesting side glens give access to the main mountain areas.

There is gabbro, considered by many rock artists to be the finest of materials, on Mull. However, it does not appear here in the spectacular forms and shapes it takes in Rhum and Skye, but only occurs as outcrops and small crags. Perhaps the best way to ascend many of the hills on the island is to link-up as many short rock pitches as possible. The side walls of gullies may be taken, as on the south face of Creach Beinn, where the beds of the gullies are at too low an angle and hold too much scree to give interesting climbing.

The gabbro first occurs in the east on Beinn Bearg, to the cast of Ben Talaidh, then following an arc westward, reappears at Beinn a'Mheadhoin, running through Corra Beinn to Cruachan Dearg, and includes part of Creach Beinn and Ben Buie to the south.

ACCOMMODATION:

Salen, where there is a good old-fashioned type of hotel, is not too far distant from Knock – 4 miles – which is a good point from which to start the ascent of Beinn Fhada and Ben More. Bicycles may be hired in Salen – useful for Loch Ba and the central group of hills.

Tobermory has several hotels, some offering hunting, fishing and shooting and riding. Reasonable accommodation is to be found at the guest house at Dervaig and the hotel at Bunessan. There is also an hotel near Fionnphort. South and westward, however, there is no accommodation until Kinloch Inn at Loch Scridain. Mull is an island on which there has been little development of the 'bed and breakfast' trade. The island has largely been taken over by immigrants. Bunessan and Fionnphort tend to be crowded with visitors to Iona.

As camping along with the rest of tourism is not yet organised either, it is still possible to make oneself at home almost anywhere on Mull. The shores of Loch na Keal, the Sound of Mull, the south coast about Carsaig and other parts have many convenient caves.

The office of the Mull Council of Social Service, The Pier, Tobermory (Tel. Tobermory 271), has lists of accommodation and provides general information, as does the Tourist Office in Oban (Tel. Oban 3122).

Centres

Salen is probably the best centre on the island for the good-living hill walker, providing the best approach to the western side of Ben More as well as approach routes through fine and varied scenery, to the central and eastern groups. From Craignure the eastern group can be best reached, and from here there is a fine high-level ridge walk southward over the tops to Tarness.

Bunessan is the best centre for exploring the Ross, and Iona when no accommodation can be had there.

The southern group can most easily be reached from Loch Buie, or the Glenmore road (map reference 622303).

EASTERN GROUP

The range between Glen Forsa and the Sound of Mull provides a fine high level ridge walk with great views over the Sound of Mull.

Beinn Chreagach Mhor (1903 ft.) is easily ascended by its north ridge from Pennygown – 3 miles. The ridge continues over **Beinn Mheadon** (2087 ft.) (pron.: Ben Moon) over **Beinn Thunicaraidh** to **Dun da Ghaoithe** (2512 ft.), pronounced 'doondagu'i'. From here the horseshoe of Choire Mhoire bends round to **Mainnir nam Faidh,** the highest hill in Mull after **Ben More** and **A'Chioch.** The name means the Castle of the Two Winds.

Of this section Campbell Steven writes: [It is] 'a grand turfy ridge steepening to form the bowl of the corrie. There is nothing dramatic about it; none of the daring architecture of Torridon or Skye. The hills of Mull are essentially places of solitude. Therein, I think, lies their great fascination. One can roam far over ridge and plateau without seeing a soul or even any sign of habitation, so few are the visitors to the high tops and so well tucked away the villages and farms.'

Mainnir Nam Fiadh (2483 ft.) 'Deerfield' – with its huge pyramid cairn, from which a descent can be made directly to Craignure in the N.N.E., or S.S.W. to a col (1600 ft.) and an ascent to Sgurr Dearg (2429 ft.)

CENTRAL GROUP

Ben Talaidh (2946 ft.) – pronounced and sometimes written 'Talla' – rises in smooth solidity when seen from the west, and, particularly from north and eastern viewpoints is a conspicuous cone seemingly far higher than it is, and thought by many to be one of the finest hills in Britain. It is bare and rocky in outline. From as far distant as South Uist it stands out and may be easily identified by its shape. Its northern spur, **Beinn Bheag,** consists of the eponymous gabbro.*

Ascending from the south-east there is an outcrop of rock on the Maol nam Faidh shoulder (the left-hand skyline seen from about 1000 ft. in Coire Ghaibhre). From here by traversing across to the north one can reach the lower rocks of a crag on the north-east face of Coire Ghaibhre. The rock and the holds are better near the bottom, where the angle is steeper. The height of the face is about 250 ft. There are pleasant clean slabs on the left of the diagonal central gully.

A descent of 1100 ft. and a turn westward leads to **Meall a'Chearraidh** (1711 ft.) and **Sgulan Mor** (1783 ft.). A hog-back ridge leads to **Cruach Choreadall** (2026 ft.) which though a fine rugged peak is outwith the gabbro circque and consists of eucrite-granite. An ascent of 400 ft. leads to the summit of **Beinn a'Mheadhoin.** A gently sloping ridge leads down to the next col of 800 ft. over which there is a path from Craig on the Coladoir river flowing into Loch Scridain, to Glen Cannel and Loch Ba' in the north. It is a steep and rough climb of 900 ft. to the top of **Corra Bheinn** (2309 ft.) – which is of the Beinn Bheag gabbro again. The olivine it contains, which is greenish in colour, tends to make the rock – like that of the Black

*The Scottish Regional Geology shows the gabbro beds only over Beinn Bheag, and round from Ben Buie to Corra Beinn.

Cuillin – sombre in colour. Also, the hills tend to be somewhat stark as neither here, nor in Skye does the rock form a soil when disintegrated, suitable for plants.

After a dip of 450 ft., a rough scramble leads to the summit of **Cruachan Dearg** (2309 ft.). When seen from the region of the ancient burial ground in the upper fork of the Glen Cannel river, this peak with Corra-Beinn and the level saddle between look like a great cathedral with balanced spires of the same height at each end.

One may descend either along the ridge over Chlachaig and an old bridle path, which, though swampy in places gives good going to Clachaig where a road is joined.

SOUTHERN GROUP

Creach Beinn (2289 ft.) which is partly of gabbro, has a number of craggy outcrops surrounding its summit and on its southern face. It is also beautifully situated above the idyllic little Loch Uisig. In the centre of the south face there is a conspicuous nose, to the left of which there are a series of slabs, rising in steps, which give some interesting and delicate climbing.

Beinn Buie (2354 ft. and 2341 ft.), pronounced Ben Buy, is separated by the deep Gleann a'Chaiginn Mhoir. It is a bold craggy face seen from Loch Buie. From Creach Beinn three rock buttresses can be seen at the top of the south face and another centrally below them.

As well as from the Loch Spelve – Loch Buie road – both tops may be reached from the Glenmore road to the north. There is a track down Gleann a'Chaiginn Mhoir from the Glenmore road (map reference 622303). It goes past Loch Airdeglais, near the south end, of which there is an interesting face on the west end of **Creag nah-Iolaire,** the western spur of Creach Bheinn.

There is a ruined castle and a complete stone circle at the hamlet of Loch Buie. The nearest bus service is to the road end in Glen More.

The south corrie of Beinn Buie is an extrusion of breccias (angular rock fragments) and ryolites (the volcanic equivalent of granite) – unfortunately from the climber's point of view. Where gabbros appear on the Geological Survey's map of the Tertiary Volcanic Districts, it forms the areas to the north, east and west of the summit, all of which are rounded hillsides with little rock extruding.

The southern crags of Creach Beinn are granophyres (which differ chiefly from granite because the quartz and felspar have interwoven – a typical hyperbasal acid intrusive rock of the Teriary period, according to Harker. The southern edge of the gabbro runs east and west some yards north of the summit.

WESTERN GROUP

Beinn Fhada (2304 ft.) is most easily approached up Gleann na Beinn Fhada and its north-western ridge. Start from the road beside Loch na Keal where the burn comes in under a bridge (map reference 507368) and head up for the pass (1750 ft.) between Beinn Fhada and Ben More, or head more directly for the summit. Wonderful views may be had of the Ben More group, especially in early morning or evening lighting in summer when parts of the mountain facing are illuminated. To the east the central Mull hills form a complex pattern, whilst northward is a view of rolling upland and the headwaters of Loch na Keal.

Ben More (3169 ft.) is the only 'Munro' in the Isles apart from those in Skye. It is probably best approached from Dishig on Loch na Keal, about 7 miles from Salen, ascending $2\frac{1}{2}$ miles straight up S.S.E. over the steepish slopes of the rocky shoulder An Gearna (1848 ft.), from which an easy ridge leads to the summit. The compass is not reliable here, or on other peaks in the island, due to magnetic rocks.

The traverse of the north-east ridge with its Cioch gives a more interesting route. It is easily reached from Glen Chlachaig or Loch na Keal.

The Cioch itself provides an enjoyable scramble. The ridge joining it to the summit of Ben More is reminiscent of the Aonach Eagach, or the Fasarinan Pinnacles of Liathach, though nowhere are the difficulties comparable. If one imagines all difficulties have been passed with the Cioch one will be in for a sharp surprise, particularly at the final summit rocks.

An easterly approach from Glen More has nothing to match the exhilarating glimpses and the sweep of the western corrie. On the south and east the great grey screes are reminiscent of a slag heap. From the Glen More side the going is not so bad if one can keep to the shoulder somewhat west of south in the direction of Maol nam Damph.

If one is making for the Inn at Kinloch some two miles can be saved by fording Loch Scridain at low tide. The view from the summit has that special quality peculiar to the island, composed of contrasts which are as much climatic as physical. As on the climb, features of land and sea seem to change from moment to moment with every foot of height gained or distance travelled. Northward are the jagged teeth of the Cuillin, with the only slightly less fierce fangs of Rhum to the left. Westward is Staffa's spectacular columnar cliff, with the interestingly shaped Treshnish Isles scattered like unstrung beads across the sea, and southward to Jura. Occasionally the low-lying coast of Ireland may be discerned. Eastward the mainland peaks of Argyll are impressive from this viewpoint, particularly in winter.

For the best view of the mountain one probably has to go to the far side of Loch na Keal, though it is hardly ever as overwhelming as Danieal depicted it from there in his charming print.

COAST

Apart from its mountains Mull offers sport to the mountaineer on its sea-cliffs. No details of routes have been sent in to the *Scottish Mountaineering Club Journal*, or have appeared – so far as is known – in any other journals. There is 'superb climbing' according to R. Chalmers and E. Thompson on the pink granite cliffs approaching 200 ft. high, at Balfour Bay, and in the region of Traigh Geal (White Strand) and on the coast around Erraid. Some of this rock is to be found, incidentally, on Iona, whence it was carried in the Ice Age. The sand rivals Calgary's for its whiteness, and the water is a limpid green.

Visitors to Mull are often told to visit Calgary Bay. It is a dull place – and the bays around the Ross are much better. Its only merit is that one may take their cars and caravans right down to the beach and camp there. The more that can be concentrated into such places the better.

The island of Erraid is accessible for two hours either side of low water, across the sands. There is no drinking water on the island. The inhabitants collect and use rainwater.

Some climbing 'punctuated by bathes' has been done on the cliffs near Quinish and Croig near Dervaig in the north-west. The rock in this region is basalt of no great height.

The Gridun sea-cliffs above the Salen – Kinloch road opposite

Inch Kenneth may yield some routes. They are of basalt, however, and the only recorded attempt to date, up a deeply-cut gully, was stopped by a large pile of 'very rotten rock'.

As the name Rudha na Uamh indicates there are several caves in the vicinity, the largest and most interesting being MacKinnon's, whereby hangs one of the tales so much detested by Macculloch . . . 'A MacKinnon, accompanied by his piper, set off to explore the cavern. They are apparently still doing so. At the time listeners heard the music grow fainter and fainter till it ceased altogether. The two have never since been seen, though sounds like pipe music, some say, periodically come from the bowels of Mull.'

It is thought to be the biggest cave in the Hebrides – longer than Fingal's and higher than the Cathedral cave of Eigg. It lies a mile south-west of Balmeanach Farm. A torch is needed and one must go at low tide. The innermost chamber is 200 yards from the entrance and small stalactites hang from its red roof.

Farther south after the road turns inland at Creach Beinn there is an area aptly named the Wilderness. Here, near the extremity of the peninsula, the top-edge of the cliff is about 1200 ft. above sea-level. A fossil tree near Rudha nan Uamba is probably the most wonderful geological sight in Mull. About 40 ft. high and three to five in diameter. The trunk is represented by a cast infilled with white trap. Another fossil tree lies toppled in a cave some distance to the north. The best guide to the site is the two waterfalls which cascade over the cliffs to the south of Rudha na Uamh, 200 yards north of Allt Airidh nan Caisteal. W. H. Murray warns that – 'The approach road from the head of Loch Scridain is the worst in Mull – four miles of mud, rock, and potholes on steep hills to Burg cottage. Two exceedingly rough miles must then be walked to the tree, and arrival timed for low water to turn a buttress of the sea-cliff.'

The Tertiary leaf-beds in the basalt cliffs at Ardtun, are of the greatest interest. The beds of fossil leaves are in a deposit of silt between basaltic sheets, formed after torrents of liquid mud had poured down the flanks of the old Mull volcano. Some of the plant varieties still recognisable are: Ginco (maiden-hair tree), Platanus (plane tree), Carylites (hazel), Onerous (oak). Along with others, including numerous conifers and angiosperms and pollen grains, suggest a climate comparable with that of the northern Mediterranean today.

ULVA

Beinn Chreagach (1025 ft.)
Beinn Eolasary (1000 ft.)
Maps: One-inch O.S., Seventh Series, sheet 45.
      Half-inch Bartholomew, sheet 47.

ACCESS:
Boat from Ulva ferry on Mull. Connected by bus to Salen via Kilmore and Gruline crossroads.

Standing westward of Mull and divided from it by scarcely a couple of hundred yards of sea, the island is wild and sparsely populated. It is mountainous throughout, its numerous gently-rounded basalt domes slightly reminiscent of the Great Pyramids. There are sea cliffs of columnar basalt. The view from the top of Beinn Eolasary is fine but the bracken is monstrous. Hordes of rabbits, lots of buzzards and several ravens have been reported here – a strange crop of fauna. The name is said to mean the Isle of Wolves.

GOMETRA

Summit 503 ft.

Gometra is connected to Ulva by a bridge, and lies to the west. A good viewpoint for the Treshnish, which are a few miles westward. Southwards and still nearer are the 'dark frowning' rocks above Gribun. **Inchkenneth** lies just south of Ulva. On it are the remains of a chapel and graveyard attributed to St. Kenneth (Cainnech), a friend of St. Columba. It is a green and fertile island and the ruins are in a good state of preservation. One of Dr. Johnson's hosts, Sir Allan MacLean, is buried in the graveyard.

Loch na Keal may be strongly commended to canoeists and sailors. Almost dividing Mull in two, it is perhaps the finest stretch of water in the island, the sail up it from seaward affording a magnificent panorama of hills that close in darkly on three sides.

EILEAN SHONA

Summit 862 ft.

Maps: One-inch O.S., Seventh Series, sheet 34.
Half-inch Bartholomew, sheet 50.

A steep and rocky island, set in the most delightful scenery. No routes.

ACCESS:

The North Channel dries at Low Water Springs. Ferry from Tioram Castle from Acharacle, Loch Shiel.

It is adjacent to Eigg rather than Mull, but may be more conveniently mentioned here. It lies in the throat of Loch Moidart, which it nearly blocks.

IONA

Dun I (332 ft.)
Carn Cul Ri Eirinn (243 ft.)

Maps: One-inch O.S., Seventh Series, sheet 51.
Half-inch Bartholomew, sheet 47.

ACCESS:

From Oban, Fort William, Tobermory by MacBraynes steamer daily except Friday and Sunday. Oban to Craignure, whence bus to Fionnphort thence ferry operated by Mr. Gibson. Tel. Fionnphort 203. Frequent service in summer time. Hires by special arrangement outside of usual steamer times.

ACCOMMODATION:

There are two hotels (open during the season), a hostel, and it is possible to stay in the monastery. When everything is full on the island there is a varied choice of hostelries nearby at Fionnphort and Bunessan. It is only necessary to go a few hundred yards westwards to find a campsite away from it all.

Dun I (*pron.:* Ee), a fine mountain in miniature. It has a north face and a chimney up it.

Carn Cul Ri Eirinn (243 ft.), 'the cairn with its back to Ireland', in the south-west of the island is traditionally the spot on which Columba resolved to give his life to Pictish evangelisation.

Eilean Didil's south face, off the west coast, will attract the climber.

There is a great deal of cliff around the island, mostly of sound rock. A complete traverse is recommended. I. Waller did it in some seven hours (*Rucksack Journal 1949*). Near the Spouting Cave on the south-west coast an overhanging cliff crossed by an incut ledge should on no account be missed.

St. Columba came to the island in 543. It seems to have been a sacred spot before he came, and for four centuries it was the centre of Celtic Christianity. The copying of books needed settled conditions. Two or three parts of Britain offered relative security from the Romans and the barbarians. Iona was one of them – secure and sacred and a more comfortable place than Skellaig Michael, a pinnacle of rock 16 miles from Ireland to which Christianity and western civilisation had clung for a hundred years.

No one knows which of the surviving Celtic Manuscripts were produced here, and which in the Northumbrian island of Lindisfarne.

The great beauty of the island, however, has nothing to do with the works of man. It seems something mainly to do with the purity of light and colour – one is forced to call it the 'atmosphere'.

Amongst others who are greatly affected by this atmosphere is Sir Kenneth Clark. In *Civilisation*, he says – 'I never come to Iona – and I used to come here almost every year when I was young – without the feeling "some god is in this place". Iona more than any other place I know gives a sense of peace and inner freedom. What does it? The light which floods around on every side. The lie of the land, which coming from the solemn hills of Mull seems strangely like Greece – like Delos even. A combination of wine-dark sea, white sand, pink granite. Or is it the memory of those holy men who for centuries kept Western civilisation alive?'

There are two main roads in Iona. One crosses the island from east to west, the other goes from the village past the cathedral to the north point.

The island is composed mostly of Lewisian gneiss, but there are also – mostly on the east – clayey beds of Torridonian age, minor igneous dykes, glacial erratics from the Ross, and raised-beach deposits of late-glacial and post-glacial age. 'Iona marble' is found in the gneiss 300 yards N.N.E. of Dun Bhuirg and at the Marble quarry on the coast at the south-east. It is also found in Tiree.

12. Treshnish Isles, looking towards Tiree and Coll.

13. Lismore. Limestone cliff.

14. *Below:* Mull. The Ben More group from Kellan, on the north side of Loch na Keal.

15. Staffa.

16. Mull. Loch Ba from Beinn a Chraig.

17. Rum. Allival from Askival and Skye Cuillin beyond.

18. Rum. Orval, north-western cliffs.

(See the excellent *Iona Past and Present* by A. and E. Ritchie, published by G. Stewart, Edinburgh, for geology, history, antiquities, birds, plants and place names, as well as a general and a geological map.)

STAFFA (Isle of Pillars)

Summit 135 ft.
Maps: One-inch O.S., Seventh Series, sheet 51
    Half-inch Bartholomew, sheet 47.

ACCESS:
From Ulva Ferry, Mull, by motor boat daily in July and August; alternate days May, June and September. Tel. C. P. Anderson, Ulva Ferry 210. MacBraynes have stopped their service as the cave is thought to be dangerous.

This small island 6 miles N.N.E. of Iona is uninhabited, but has been much visited by tourists since it came to fame in the late eighteenth century. Sir Joseph Banks is blamed for misnaming Uamh-binn (the cave of melody) Fingal's Cave, and Mendelsson made a sort of musical Malapropism out of it. There are scores of old prints of Staffa; Daniel did several.

The cave is 200 ft. long and 60 ft. high and the water about 60 ft. deep at the entrance. There are other fine caves which might be explored in a boat. J. Dunn who went through Corrievrecken in his canoe also visited Staffa by the same means. He intended to return to Iona the same day. Though dead calm on his outward trip, he was stormbound for a week before it was possible to return.

TRESHNISH ISLES

Lunga (337 ft.)
Bac Mor (The Dutchman's Cap) (284 ft.)
Carn a Burgh Mor (112 ft.)
Maps: One-inch O.S., Seventh Series, sheet 44.
    Half-inch Bartholomew, sheet 47.

ACCESS:

By motor-boat from Ulva Ferry, Mull, Wednesdays and Fridays or by special arrangement with C. P. Anderson, Ulva Ferry. Also from Fionnphort, Mr. Gibson. Tel. 203.

Lunga has a cliff on the west side and close to it is Dun Cruit or 'Harp Rock'. It is steep-sided, but with a possible line of ascent up a crack on its north side. The gap is about 12 ft. at the top, about 100 ft. above the water. Around Lunga are a number of small islands, among them Carn a Burgh Mor and Carn a Burgh Beag. On Burgh Mor is the ruin of one of the strongholds of the chiefs of Macleans. Perched on a crag, it had only one entrance by a precipitous path.

The Treshnish Isles are quite uninhabited, and are interesting to the ornithologist for the great number of seabirds which frequent them during the nesting season.

They are a few miles to the west of Ulva, in the Passage of Tiree, Bac Mor and Bac Beag lying furthest into the Atlantic. They have cattle. The smaller islets are Sgeir a Chaisteil (Castle Rock), Sgeir an Fheoir (Grass Island) and Fladda, where a lobster fisher generally spends the summer.

REFERENCES:

Tour to the Hebrides with Dr. Johnson, Boswell.

J. Macculloch, op. cit., Vol. iv, p. 228. Iona, etc., Vol. iv, p. 146.

British Regional Geology: Scotland; The Tertiary Volcanic Districts 1948. (H.M.S.O.)

'*Good Words*'. *Iona*, by the Duke of Argyll, 1869.

Iona Past and Present, A. E. Ritchie. Pub. Stewart, Edinburgh.

The Island Hills, Campbell Steven.

Farmer in the Western Isles, MacKenzie.

Kidnapped, R. L. Stevenson.

Scottish Mountaineering Club Journal – contains several articles in early numbers relating to Ben More, also:

Vol. 15, p. 30, Eilean na Cloiche, by A. Arthur, 1917.

15, p.284, Carn a Burgh Mor.

16, p.122, Mountaineering in Iona, by Fraser Campbell.

29, p.239, Dun Da Ghaoithe, by R. North.

4

Rum

Barkeval (1924 ft.)
Allival (2365 ft.)
Askival (2659 ft.)
Trallval (2300 ft.)
Ashval (2442 ft.) named Ainsval by O.S.
Sgurr nan Gillean (2503 ft.)
Ruinsival (1607 ft.)

Maps: One-inch O.S., Seventh Series, sheet 33.
      Half-inch Bartholomew, sheet 50.

ACCESS:

Rum is controlled by the Nature Conservancy. Mallaig is the nearest port on the mainland, whence there is a regular service four days per week (not Tuesdays, Fridays or Sundays) to the island. A boat may be hired from Bruce Watt, Mallaig.

The pier at Kinloch is now available for the landing of visitors. The weather has to be very calm before landings can be made elsewhere, either at Harris Bay on the west coast or Bagh na h-Uamha on the east. It may be possible for a party to hire a boat from Glen Brittle, Skye, or Canna. Enquiries should be made at the Post Office at both places. Harris is a suitable place from which to attack Ruinsival, and Bagh na h-Uamha is the nearest landing that can be made for an approach to the ridges. Loch Scresort and Canna harbour are the only good anchorages.

Permission to visit the island during the holiday periods should be obtained well in advance from the Nature Conservancy, 12 Hope Terrace, Edinburgh 9, through the secretary of one's club. It is agreed that there should be no rescue liability falling on the island's estate staff, and that climbers will comply with such guidance as may be given them from time to time about particular places within the mountain area which must be avoided for scientific reasons, or periods when the island has to be closed to visitors.

'To minimise disturbance of scientific work,' says the Official

Guide, 'permission to stay on Rhum [Ordnance Survey Spelling] will be granted only to scientists, naturalists and qualified mountaineers' – others should not be too alarmed and despondent.

The privacy of the island, one might say virginity, used to be a stimulus to visit it. Now that the owner is no longer a private, but is a public authority, and the regulations which are the same for all have replaced the old system of privilege, applicants may find the air has been let out of their egos when told they must wait till the Girl Guide campers have gone.

The Conservators are patient, long-suffering men. They know that although we don't go to their island to make whoopee, they take us for decent but ignorant folk who can soon create a lot of damage. They manage, advise and clear-up. They are doing their best to educate us. There are blue areas for bipeds and green areas for quadrupeds, day visitors and picknickers; trails with authorised stopping points, where on the pretext of admiring the wonders of the beaches or bogs the aged and weary may pause and gasp with appreciation.

ACCOMMODATION:
There is none, officially. Usually it is best to camp. It may be possible occasionally to obtain permission to use the three or four deserted buildings scattered around the island – entirely unofficially. A bothy at Dibidil has been repaired and renovated.

ROADS AND PATHS:
The only roads on the island are from Kinloch to Harris, east to west across the island with a branch northward to Kilmory. The Dibidil path starts at a gate in the deer fence close to the jetty at Scresort. It rises to 750 ft. before descending to Glen Dibidil, 5 miles, but demands a great deal less climbing than an attempt to follow the sea-cliffs; and offers much easier going than the tussocky moor. From Dibidil it rises again to 500 ft. in the 2½ miles to Papadil, being rather more indistinct. From Papadil to Glen Harris there is no track and one must maintain a height of about 600 ft. to avoid the sea-cliffs. The west of the island may be approached from the Kinloch–Harris–Kilmory road junction. From there a stalker's path goes to the bealach at the top of Glen Guirdil, and thence round under the basalt summit cliff of Orval, on to Bloodstone hill, otherwise called Creag nan Stardean (1273 ft.) and the fine sea-cliffs of Sgor Mhor.

The island consists of a square platform of purple-red Torridonian sandstone, 500 to 1000 ft. high, fringed with sea-cliffs in most places. From this south of the Kinloch-Harris line rises the main range which, like Skye is called the Cuillin. The northern peaks – Allival, Askival and Trallval consist of rock allied to gabbro, but with fewer basalt dykes. Ashval and Sgurr nan Gillean are capped by quartz-felsite overlying Torridonian. On the south and west there is some granite, which provides good hill-walking as in the Cairngorms, rising to 1875 ft. at Orval.

Climbing

Though the traverse of the main ridge is nowhere as difficult as that of Skye, and if two or three boulder problems are avoided, involves no 'climbing', it is yet to be rated as one of the classic mountaineering expeditions.

Beyond Askival is one of the wildest, loneliest and most deeply cut glens in Scotland, Glen Dibidil, which runs down to the sea opposite Eigg, and is a haunt of the golden eagle. To walk the ridges of Rum from Allival round to Sgurr nan Gillean and, descending thence to Glen Dibidil, and return along the coast to the landing-bay is a rare day, a great day and one which will stand out in the memory as a unique experience.

Eight or nine hours are needed for the round trip from Kinloch over the summits to **Sgurr nan Gillean** and back, either by the path from Dibidil or returning to the Ashval–Trallval bealach (1730 ft.) along the ridge. The traverse along the east flank of **Trallval** to the Bealach an Oir (1550 ft.) is easy. From here the west route round **Askival** and **Allival** is quicker, but the east side more picturesque. The ascent to the Askival–Beinn nan Stac bealach involves about 100 ft. of climbing, thence a descent into the Coire nan Ghrunnd which ends at 1350 ft. below the end of Askival's east ridge. The most direct way back to Kinloch is by the Dibidil path, which is indistinct at this point and may easily be overshot.

If taking the other route from Bealach an Oir, descend 250 ft. directly into Coire Rangill, then traverse at about 1300 ft. and re-ascend to the Allival–Barkival bealach, and so down to the Slugan burn (2 hours from Bealach an Oir).

Papadil to Kinloch over all the main tops takes about 6 hours.

Barkeval (1924 ft.) is the northernmost hill of the main range. It is easily reached from Kinloch and its summit commands a good view of the island. If one takes the Harris road out of Kinloch a gate gives access to a track through the woods behind the house until the Slugan burn can be found, which one can follow for about 1000 ft.

This slope is a mass of primroses and other wild flowers in the spring, which grow almost to summit level.

The crags on the south can be reached from Glen Harris, down Broad Buttress – the westernmost – or by going down west from the summit by a terrace and cutting back under the top rocks and above a band of rock and the more broken rocks west of it.

From the terrace a conspicuous green patch to the left of a 'waterslide' is a good landmark (the **Western Isles Buttress** is to the right of it and **Rose Root** left, as seen from below).

Western Isles Buttress, 350 ft., Difficult, – the buttress left of the 'waterslide' (cairn at the start), goes to the top left of a 'rectangle' and follows the best line to the top.

Broad Buttress, 450 ft., Moderate, is the buttress right of the waterslide whose base forms the top edge of the 'rectangle'. Not as fine as it looks and lines can be taken at will. It is a possible line of descent from the summit. The wall on the east, although steep, might make a good face route starting from the gully.

Narnis Arête, 350 ft., Difficult, starts at the top right of the 'rectangle' on Broad Buttress and gives scrambling to a cairn where the ridge becomes an arête.

Rose Root Slab and Crack, 260 ft., Severe, though short is probably the best route so far on the face. It starts west of Western Isles Buttress, where there is a bay with a 60-ft. slab to the left. Climb the slab, which is steeper than it looks, and continue for 20 ft. on the same line to an overhanging nook. One can continue straight up by the left side of the nook, taking the overhangs directly – 60 ft., Hard Severe – or break out right to grassy ledges (just left of 'Green Patch'), then right, up a small slab under a face to base of deeply-cut chimney – 50 ft. Fine crux. Then 60 ft. straight up from stony shelf to top.

Allival (2365 ft.) can be reached by either the Slugan or Dibidil paths. The escarpments which encircle the summit, except on the south, are of allivalite, a pale variety of gabbro, while the slopes between are of peridotite, a dark variety, which weathers orange-brown. Allivalite, though of a different hue, is otherwise very similar to the black gabbro of the Skye Cuillin and is just as rough and hard. It weathers into bold pinnacles and affords fine footing to the climber. The north ridge is easy, if the summit cliffs are avoided by a gully to the right. It can also be climbed straight up (Moderate).

On the east face there are two long scarps which give routes of about 100 ft. in length.

The *East Ridge* is the right hand skyline seen from Askival. It gives a climb of Very Difficult standard.

The *Oxford Groove*, 200 ft., Severe, cleaves both tiers immediately south of the East Ridge. Below Oxford Groove there is a rib and a slabby right wall – *Choochter Rib*, 200 ft., Very Difficult. Start at the lowest rocks. Keep close to rib. Climb 10 ft. slab on right and gain ledge on left. Mantelshelf on to flake on nose. An awkward move on to a ledge into an overhung recess (60 ft.) leads to a short chimney, then right and up crest (50 ft.).

Seen from the floor of Coire nan Ghrunnd, the upper cliffs of the south-east face consist of three main tiers:

1. *Summit Tier:* This stands well back from the top of the middle tier and is only about 40 ft. high at its left-hand (west) end, diminishing to a rocky step above the Allival Slab (on the flank of the East Ridge).

2. *Middle Tier:* This is the broadest and most continuous of the three bands of rock stretching from the South Ridge (above the bealach from Askival) to the Allival Slab. It may be divided into three sections:

(*a*) Left-hand section, from the South Ridge to an obvious V-gully, above the main scree shoot and also cleaving the bottom tier.
(*b*) Central section, from the V-gully bounding the Allival Slab on the left.
(*c*) Right-hand section. The Allival Slab and eastward.

3. *Bottom Tier:* is a broad steeply-sloping ledge of grass and scree and only offers worthwhile climbing below Oxford Groove (q.v.) and Allival Slab. A number of routes of varying degrees of severity of under 100 ft. have been done on it.

On the Middle Tier there is a 200 ft. Mild Severe route called

Lotus. Around the corner from the Allival Slab there are three grooves. Take the leftmost.

Cambridge Arête is immediately left of Oxford Groove. Up blocks left of overhang, then by a deep 12 ft. groove, and traverse to arête. Forty ft. up arête and finish by awkward crack. Severe.

To the left of Cambridge Arête is *Flake and Crack Route*, 115 ft., Very Difficult. Start a third of the way along a corner on the Allival Slab. Climb right to big flake and on to slab. Finish straight up by obvious crack.

Askival (2659 ft.) is the highest point, and provides more climbing than any other mountain on the island. It has a sharp north ridge, a steep east ridge, and a buttress on the north-east some 250-ft. high. The North Ridge, connecting with Allival is three-quarters of a mile long. To follow the crest affords some 600 ft. of scrambling. In the middle of the ridge is the Askival Pinnacle – which is really a step – which can be easily turned on the east side. Taken directly it is moderate. The 30-ft. gully on the western side provides another moderate line to the top.

On the west face of the North Ridge there is a route – *Zig-Zag*, 120 ft., Hard Severe, on the buttress to the right of the gully leading to the right (North end of level stretch of ridge north of Askival Pinnacle). Start at lowest rocks up rightwards cracks to avoid overhang. Back left (delicate) and follow edge overlooking gully to stance at start of wide ledge. Follow right till it is possible to climb upwards to North Ridge.

The East Ridge is easy, though it steepens near the top where it meets the summit crags. There is a 'difficult' variation on the north side of the ridge, starting at an easy gully. The route follows the line of a groove above a small cave.

Between the East and South Ridges is a rock-face on which numerous climbs have been done. It is on the flank of the spur which extends eastwards below the foot of East Ridge proper, at approximately 1500 ft.

There are various lines about very difficult standard of around a hundred feet in length. They have been marked with cairns, arrows and other graffiti. The best route is probably *The Candle*, 140 ft., Mild Severe. About the centre of the face there is a tall pillar in a niche. Climb the left crack of The Candle. Move right and climb

19. *Overleaf:* Pinnacle on Orval.

20. *Above:* Rum. Sgor Mhor sea cliffs.

crack to ledge and belay (70 ft.). Corner above avoided on left to grass terrace (70 ft.). Climb may be continued up the Upper Tier (100 ft. Difficult).

Farther left the line of cliffs is broken by a grass slope and stream before it continues leftward. Near the right edge of the buttress is a deep, narrow trap chimney (cairn and arrow) 190 ft. Very Difficult. Climb to ledge on left (60 ft.). Continue up fault above, passing under two large chockstones.

Fluch, 200 ft., Very Difficult, is about 30 ft. left of Trap Chimney. Climb crack to ledge and belay (strenuous). Continue up corner to belay on grass ledge under twin cracks (70 ft.). Up right-hand crack and into bay on left (50 ft.). Climb corner to top.

Fuarr, 210 ft., Difficult. About 30 ft. left of Fluch (arrow). Up slab to corner. Climb right-hand crack to large grass ledge and belay (100 ft.). From ledge above trend left over slabs.

The South Ridge can be followed without difficulty from Askival's summit to **Beinn nan Stac** (1730 ft.). Overlooking the lochan of Coire nan Ghrunnd, on the north flank of the spur which extends east from below the foot of the East Ridge proper (i.e. on the opposite side, and at about the same height as the south-east crags) is an escarpment of small cliffs. At the left-hand end is an obvious buttress split by two prominent cracks. The left-hand crack (arrow) is *Calder Chimney*, 110 ft., Very Difficult. The right-hand: *Fylde Crack*, 130 ft., Very Difficult.

Striding Edge, 100 ft., Very Difficult, starts at a slabby arête about 20 yards to the right of Fylde Crack. All the starting points have been marked by arrows.

The West Ridge from Bealach an Oir is easy, except for the summit escarpment which can be turned on the south side.

On the North-West Buttress there are a lot of good routes, especially on the portion south of the Askival Pinnacle, where it is fairly sound gabbro and about 250 ft. high – The Edinburgh Climb and the Atlantic Ridge on this buttress are both claimed to be 350 ft. in length. At the other end of the scale routes of under 40 ft. in length on this face have been described in the Journal.

Botterill of the Yorkshire Ramblers is given credit for being the first to climb on what the old islands Guide called 'this huge buttress'. He said it was, '—a replica in miniature of the Slanting Gully of Lliwedd'.

The Edinburgh Climb, 350 ft., Severe, lies on the part of the

Buttress facing almost north which can be seen from the North Ridge. Cairn at start. Easy rock for 15 ft., then groove (crux), traverse to shelf and belay. Then line of least resistance to summit. No escape possible. First ascent: Nicol, Smart and Slesser.

The 200 ft. *Askival Slab* has been climbed by the left edge and up a corner on the right.

No. 1 Gully is 20 yards to the south of the corner of the Buttress. The rock is trap. Escape (moderate) can be made on either side. It contains a chockstone pitch (Difficult).

No. 2 Gully farther south is wide and rotten.

No. 1–2 Gully, between, is moderate.

Atlantic Ridge, 350 ft., Very Difficult, is the right-hand rib of two which are clearly seen when the N.W. Buttress is viewed from Trallval. Start at cairn a few feet right of sharp left-hand edge. Follow shallow crack for 90 ft. to a platform on left-hand ridge. The route continues a few yards to the right up a very steep 50 ft. wall. Thereafter the climb goes all the way to the top, and ends suddenly at the summit, according to W. H. Murray, the author.

Trallval (2300 ft.). At Askival the main ridge turns west to the Bealach an Oir (1500 ft.) and then rises to Trallval, a finely-shaped peak, especially when viewed from Dibidil. It has two tops close together, the westernmost being slightly higher.

Apart from the route along the main ridge, Trallval can be reached by following the road to the head of Glen Kinloch, then turning due south and following the Amhainn Sgathaig until Trallval can be gained. From Dibidil the way is obvious, though from either bealach some scrambling may be necessary.

The West Corrie. Low down in the corrie, and a short way below the west side of Bealach an Fhuarain, is a gabbro wall 300 yards long and 400 ft. high called Harris Buttress. On the south flank of the Corrie's north wall are two peridotite outcrops. The one nearest to the west end is called the Triangular Buttress.

At the centre of Harris Buttress there is a not very definite rib, below which a rock is poised like a capstan. Shallow gullies run up on either side of the rib, each with a large overhang. About 50 ft. to the right of the right-hand gully there is a vertical crack about 250 ft. high. About 40 ft. to the right of the crack, a shallow and broken depression runs up the rocks, leading to the start of *Archangel Route*, a 400 ft. Very Difficult, by Michael Ward and W. H. Murray. About 60 ft. up at the top left of the depression, there is a block-pinnacle, the base of which is so badly shattered that a direct approach from below looks highly dangerous. Climb the rocks on the left of the depression to a platform at the left side of the pinnacle. Scramble over the top of the pinnacle, 'spread the wings of faith', and take a short, bold flight across the gap to a chimney on the right-hand side of the depression. The chimney becomes a vertical crack of 20 ft. with good holds. Follow a broad ledge rightwards and turn a corner into a little bay beneath a great groove. Go 20 ft. up the groove, then climb up leftwards on to a narrow ledge. Follow the ridge directly upwards till it falls back among broad slabs which steepen into a line of overhangs running across the buttress. Climb diagonally up to the left, aiming for a sharp, steep corner, where a delightful climb is had up an exposed but rough gabbro slab.

The *Centre Rib*, another long route of character and great interest (Severe) was climbed by D. Bennet and D. Stewart.

Triangular Buttress of Trallval. The main features are a central gully, wide, wet and broken, and to the right a high-angled slab, about 100 ft. high and 150 ft. across.

Ptarmigan Crack, 150 ft., Difficult. Follows the chimney forming the right side of the triangle.

Fat Man's Evasion, Severe. Starts 80 ft. left of the previous crack. An airy traverse leads across right to the upper part of the chimney.

Bloodstone Crack, 100 ft., Very Severe. To the left of the Central Gully is a steep, short crack. Cairn. The start is strenuous and goes by the right wall.

After Trallval there is no more gabbro. The descent down to the Bealach an Fhuarain (1730 ft.) between Trallval and Ashval is an easy scramble, if obvious difficulties are avoided.

Ashval (2552 ft.) can be climbed straight up its North Ridge from the Bealach an Fhuarain. Half-way up this ridge becomes a narrow arête of rather loose and slippery rock. The normal route is on the west face. Considerable difficulty was experienced by a party descending these rocks in winter conditions, the standard being estimated at about Very Difficult. A fairly long detour is necessary to either side if all difficulty is to be avoided. In descending from Ashval on the Dibidil side of this ridge one should leave the ridge-line almost at its top. From Ashval to Sgurr nan Gillean is a fairly level walk of about a mile. Between is an unnamed top (2475 ft.). From it runs a long and interesting ridge westward to Ruinsival (1607 ft.).

The cliffs of the Glen Dibidil side (east) of these mountains are of various types of rough igneous rocks, with numerous grassy ledges.

On the East Ridge of Ashval, between 1000 and 1250 ft. is a buttress like the Douglas Boulder on a small scale. A 250 ft. route on good rock was done here by J. G. Parish. It lies to the left of two parallel grassy gullies. At one point above, the ridge is exposed and narrow.

Sgurr Nan Gillean (2503 ft.) has a steep cliff 200–300 ft. high below the summit on the Glen Dibidil side. This side is to be avoided in descent. The best way off is probably from a point half-way along the track from Papadil to Dibidil.

Papadil is a most attractive and romantically lonely spot. The small fresh-water loch is backed by a wood of mixed trees.

Ruinsival has on its north-west side above Glen Harris, several buttresses fairly low on the hillside where there is good rock-climbing. Situated as they are they are suitable for a time when the clouds are as low as 1000 ft. A disadvantage is the distance from Kinloch.

The left-hand profile is the **Giant's Staircase**, a series of nine rock steps leading from about 1000 ft. to the summit. At the fifth step is a 70 ft. pinnacle. Severe by the face, Very Difficult by the chimney behind. From the top of the pinnacle, step off on to a steep 20 ft. wall. 250 ft. of Moderate to Difficult climbing leads to the top up the remaining steps.

The Lower Buttress lies about 100 yards below and to the right of the bottom of the Staircase, Woden's Wall is a steep face to the right and a little above the last. Above is the Upper Tier about 150 ft. high. From left to right on it are No. 1 arête, No. 1. Gully, and so on. Between is the Middle Tier. On this face new routes have proliferated.

Like this rock face, the editor was in tears before he had sorted out claims to new short routes and the confusion in naming them. Only those exceeding 60 ft. can be mentioned.

Across the big stone shoot to the right of the Middle Tier is a

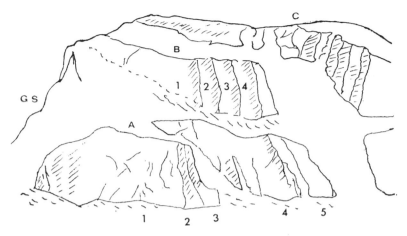

Fig. 2 RUINSIVAL North-West Cliffs

GS – Giant's Staircase

A – Lower Tier
   1. North Buttress

   2. Woden's Wall
   3. Thor's Buttress
   4. Frigga's Buttress
   5. South Buttress

B – Middle Tier
   1. Left Wall
   2. 3 & 4. Grooves and arêtes

C – Summit Tier
Green Wall is across the stone shoot to
the right of the Middle Tier

considerable area of rock easily distinguished by the big green plat-form in its centre. It is suggested that this be called Green Wall, on which is the Face Route, 200 ft., Severe. The start (cairn) lies 25 ft. left of the rake leading left to the Green Platform at the foot of a trap-dyke. Go left by a crack to a ledge and follow further cracks to the top.

Right Corner (160 ft., Very Difficult). The far right corner of Green Wall has a tongue of slabs with an undercut crack right. Climb slabs beside crack.

Right Corner Chimney (135 ft., Difficult). Chimney bounding slabs on right.

Middle Tier, North Section
No. One Arête (180 ft., M.S.). Start at lowest point of arête and scramble to where rock steepens. Climb straight up overhang and over pedestal to final grooves.

85

Seoras (150 ft., V.S.). On the right of the Upper Buttress is a dark depression crossed by a narrow trap dyke. Climb to apex of triangle and over overhang to gain groove. Fork right near top to finish at top of *No. One Arête*.

REFERENCES:

Apart from various pamphlets published by The Nature Conservancy, Edinburgh –
Macculloch, op. cit., Vol. iv, p. 217 ff.
The Cruise of The Betsy, Hugh Miller, 1858.
British Regional Geology, Scotland: The Tertiary Volcanic Districts, (H.M.S.O.), 1948.
The Scottish Mountaineering Club Journal:
　Vol.　1, p. 259, Rum, by Sir Hugh Munro.
　　　10, p.　26, Geology, by A. Harker. Rum, by E. Hodge.
　　　24, p.　　9, A Camp on Rum, by T. Weir.
　　　24, p.　42, The Mountains of Rum, by J. G. Parish.

NEW CLIMBS:
　Vol. 22, p.　69.
　　　24, p. 133, (by W. H. Murray and M. Ward).
　　　24, p. 327, (by W. H. Murray and J. G. Parish).
　　　27, p. 267, 280.
　　　29, p.　51.
Yorkshire Rambler's Club Journal, Vol. V., p. 32.
Oxford Mountaineering, 1935, 1937.
Fell and Rock Journal, 1946, 'Raid on Rhum', F. Jenkins.
Junior Mountaineering Club of Yorkshire, 'Guide to the Island of Rhum,' 1946.
Edinburgh University Mountaineering Club Journal, summer 1947 and winter 1947.
M.A.M. Journal, 1966. Climbing in Rum (Offprints from Miss A. Littlejohn, Vet.Lab., Weybridge, Surrey).

5

Ardnamurchan to Cape Wrath

Part I – The Small Isles

The Parish of the Small Isles comprises Rum, Eigg, Muck, Canna and the uninhabited rocks of Umaolo and Oighskeir (Hyskeir). These isles lie between Ardnamurchan and the South of Skye.

The islands neighbouring Skye: – the Ascrib group, Soay, Scalpay, Pabbay, Raasay, South Rona and Trodday, are dealt with in the *Island of Skye* District Guide.

EIGG (A Hollow)

Beinn Blaudhe (974 ft.)
An Cruachan (982 ft.)
Beinn Tighe (1034 ft.)
Sgurr of Eigg (1289 ft.)

Maps: One-inch O.S., Seventh Series, sheet 34.
Half-inch Bartholomew, sheet 50.

ACCESS:

Steamer service from Mallaig by MacBraynes, Monday, Wednesday and Thursday. Saturday service is provided by Bruce Watt, Mallaig. At Eigg the steamer lies off Castle Island and passengers transfer to a ferry-boat. The excursion return fare of 12s. 6d. should make this island appeal to the parsimonious.

It is also possible to make the short sea crossing from Rhu Arisaig pier by hiring the ferry-boat (*Roddie Campbell, Cuagach, Eigg 14*), or the estate launch (*The Factor, Eigg 3*). These boats are available to visit other islands. There is a mini-bus and cars for hire on the island.

ACCOMMODATION:

Full board is provided at Laig Farm (Mrs. D. Kirk). There are also a number of cottages to let, and two caravans. Particulars may be obtained from the Factor and Angus Mackinnon, Cleadale. Permission may be obtained to use an old cow-shed a short distance up the road from Galmisdale or a fine bothy at Bidean Boidheach.

'Eigg is a lovely little island,' writes Hugh MacDiarmid, 'with its great cockscomb of a Sgurr; a fertile island, with a kindly climate; profuse with the little white rose of Scotland; and with singing sands on its western coast.'

Eigg is four miles in length and three in breadth. It is composed of two hill-masses connected by a neck of low ground. The Scuir, a unique ridge or rampart of columnar pitchstone porphyry, rests upon the southmost hilly mass like a gigantic prehistoric beast, and forms a notable landmark.

The Scuir of Eigg

A fine miniature mountain and the highest point on the island, is almost completely encircled by cliffs. On the east face the cliffs reach maximum height in a fantastic overhanging nose (c. 500 ft.) which appears completely uncompromising. There are one or two attractive possibilities on the north side: a moderate zig-zag route – not recommended in wet conditions – 200 yards right of the Nose. The splendidly situated South Wall is a great rampart about a mile long, broken by easy grassy gullies to the west.

H. MacInnes and I. Clough have come closest to a direct ascent of the Nose taking a line a few feet to its left, following an obvious crack line, tending out rightwards. The exposure was extreme and the rock loose.

The following four climbs are on the long face to the left of the Nose, before the first gully leading to the summit ridge. This section is cut across by Long Ledge at a little less than half height and below the steepest part of the face. The upper wall, on this section, is split into three by two deep recesses, Collie's Cleft and Botterill's Crack (see diagram). All were first ascents by I. Clough and party.

South Wall – Collie's Cleft, 200 ft., Severe.

This climb follows the large corner recess immediately west of the columnar wall which bounds the Nose. Gain it by obvious heather gully, the entry to which is awkward.

At the back of the corner a deep chimney leads to a ledge and belays (80 ft.). Continue up vertical left chimney which has a most unpleasant exit (120 ft.).

Eagle Chimney, 250 ft., Hard Severe.

There are several crack and chimney lines on the wall between Collie's Cleft and Botterill's Crack. Eagle Chimney is near the centre of the wall and prominent. There is another chimney farther right which becomes more distinct higher up. Eagle Chimney is most distinct in its lower half. Gain start by approach to Botterill's Crack and walk rightwards across Long Ledge.

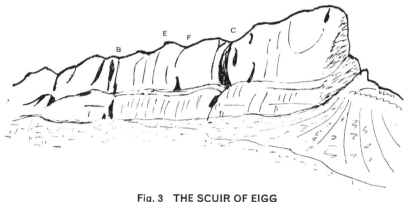

Fig. 3   THE SCUIR OF EIGG

B – Botterill's Crack   E – Eagle Chimney   F – The Flue   C – Collie's Cleft

Climb the chimney, the first pitch of which is continuously difficult (110 ft.). The best climb on Eigg to date.

The Flue, 270 ft., Very Severe.

This is the chimney right of Eagle Chimney, most distinct in its upper half. Approach via Long Ledge. Climb heathery rocks and gain base of chimney (35 ft.). Follow shallow chimney, then steep wall on right which leads to restricted stance at back of second chimney (70 ft.). Up chimney on good holds to terrace (80 ft.), then trend left up pleasant slabs to top (85 ft.).

Botterill's Crack, 170 ft., Severe.

A heather gully leads to a big bay at the level of the Long Ledge. In the bay are three well-defined chimneys and cracks, and two further chimney lines start some way up the left wall. The climb follows the left-hand of the three main lines. Recommended.

Northern Eigg

There is an almost continuous line of cliffs on the east, north and west faces of the moorland plateau which fills the centre of the northern half of the island. Extending for about six miles, they vary in height between 100 and 500 ft. For the most part they are disappointing, being broken into tiers by grass ledges. However, there are two very impressive sections of cliff (on the north and east faces) which might repay further investigation. The following are on the west face, overlooking the Bay of Laig and Cleadale.

Cleadale Face: The most prominent feature of this face is a tall pillar culminating in a crazy pinnacle. Laig Buttress is a clean flying buttress on the extreme right. There is a small Sphinx-like pinnacle to its right and a pleasant little rock amphitheatre behind.

Laig Buttress – Grit, 150 ft., Severe.

From a cairn, climb groove to ledge (Peg Belay, 40 ft.). Move up right into corner, up into overhanging niche on left, and swing up left again to stance (Peg Belay, 60 ft.). Continue to top. (A bold line – Ed.)

The Pod – 150 ft., Very Severe.

Start at broken groove 30 ft. left of Grit. Climb groove which culminates in short overhanging corner crack – crux. Easier to top.

The rocks of the 'flying buttress' were found to be loose and vegetatious.

There are numerous fissures down the centre of the pinnacle. Some were explored from above and though deep, none gave a through route.

Poll nam Partan Crags – overlooking bay of Poll nam Partan (N. of Galmisdale pier). Though short (70 ft.) they are steep, and broken into numerous cracks and chimneys which provide climbing similar to gritstone.

General

The traverse of the summit plateaux of either the Scuir or the northern hills of Eigg is a very pleasant and interesting expedition. The summit ridge of the Scuir is quite rugged, particularly towards its eastern end where one has a fine sense of exposure. The wild flowers, which include campion, thyme, willow, golden rod and a giant heather, though not very diverse in kinds, grow profusely and to an unusually large size.

There is a fossilised coniferous tree trunk to be found just to the right of the foot of Botterill's Crack on the South Face of the Scuir. According to Harker the Scuir at one stage nourished at least one small glacier. It flowed down from the most noticeable gap in the south-west escarpment, and its terminal moraine, composed of blocks of pitchstone, some of huge size, is seen streaming down to the coast.

The island of Oigh-sgeir (Huskeir) 18 miles west-north-west from Eigg, is pitchstone identical with that of the Scuir and probably once continuous with it. In many places, particularly around the coast, a pure black glassy selvage which has been extruded through the volcanic layers, may be found.

The Cave of Francis, where in 1577 the Macleods suffocated 395 local Macdonalds, is a mile from the harbour on the south shore. Go up the road marked 'private' and climb the first stile on the left, follow a path to the cottage and then along a sheep track till you come to a cliff fence. Go along this to a zig-zag track leading to the shore beside a small burn. Turn left to the Massacre cave and right to Cathedral cave. The latter is still used for Catholic services, the custom originating in the time of persecution after the '45.

From An Cruachan to Bein Bhuidhe is a fine walk with the mountains of Rum dominating the lower line of Barra and Uist farther out to the west. With the numerous sea-birds around, either on the wing, or, such as the shear-waters, resting on the sea, it is similar to a sea-cliff that has receded a mile or so from the coast. From the north-west flank of Bein Bhuidhe one can descend by the gently graded track that was made for the ponies to bring down the peat.

Fossil reptile and fish are to be found in shale just above low-water mark at the north end at Eilean Tuilm.

The sands in the bay north of Laig, which are composed of quartz crystals, emit sound similar to an Aeolian harp if one walks across them at times of change of temperature.

A Gaelic account of the earliest known meeting of the island chiefs, after they had become subject to the Scottish Crown, seems to indicate it took place in Eigg, and not in Islay, although the wording is obscure.

(—at Kildonnan in Eigg, where the staff of Lordship of Clanranald was given to one who was nominated Macdonnall and Donald of Isla.)

MUCK (Isle of Pigs)

Ben Aerean (451 ft.)

Maps: One-inch O.S., Seventh Series, sheet 34.
Half-inch Bartholomew, sheet 50.

ACCESS:
Visitors to Muck normally disembark at Eigg (q.v.). and are met by motor-launch.

ACCOMMODATION:
There is no full board provided, but there are three cottages to let. Application should be made to L. MacEwan, Isle of Muck. Camping is allowed with permission, and a barn is normally available in bad weather.

Ben Aerean is an easy climb from Gallanach. There is a steep cliff on the south-west side above the bay of Camus Mor.

The greater part of the island consists of sheet basalt giving it the typical form and outline of dark cliffs in terraces with grassy ledges and flattish crowns. Dolerite dykes are common in Muck running north-west to south-east.

A few alpine plants grow here, 2000 ft. below their usual level. The list is a short one – dwarf juniper, crowberry, club moss, rose root sedum, mountain cats-paw, pyramidal bugle.

CANNA

Carn a Ghaill (690 ft.)
Compass Hill (458 ft.)

Maps: One-inch O.S., Seventh Series, 33.
Half-inch Bartholomew, 50

ACCESS:

The same steamers that serve the other Small Isles call at Canna (q.v. Eigg). Although there is a pier, passengers are transferred to and from ship by ferry-boat.

Apart from Carn a Ghaill and Compass Hill – so named because it upsets them – there is an isolated stack on the shore a quarter of a mile north of the harbour where a Clanranald chief imprisoned his wife. Of it, Sir Walter Scott says:

> 'Seek not the giddy crag to climb
> To view the turret scathed by time:
> It is a task of doubt and fear
> To aught but goat or mountain deer.'

He is probably right. The rock is conglomerate. There has been no ascent recorded.

There are the remains of a cashel or nunnery, $2\frac{1}{2}$ miles west of the harbour. Sgeir nam Ban Naomha (The Skerry of the Holy Women) is probably named after it. The sculptured stone cross at A'Chill is quite close to the ruins of St. Columba's Chapel, above the harbour.

The island of Sanda is connected to Canna by a bridge.

Dun Channa, the westernmost tip of the island, was fortified by a wall.

SHIANT ISLANDS

Garbh Eilean Summit (528 ft.)

Maps: One-inch O.S., Seventh Series, sheet 18.
Bartholomew half-inch, sheet 57.

ACCESS:

Hires from Tarbert, Harris and Scalpay may be arranged with N. MacLeod & Sons, Harbour View, Scalpay. Tel. Scalpay 209. The Shiants are about $4\frac{1}{2}$ miles south-east from Park in Lewis, separated by the Sound of Shiant.

The three principal islands, Garbh Eilean, Eilean an Tighe and Eilean Mhuire are all uninhabited. The two first mentioned are connected by a neck. The scenery is grand but the rock being columnar basalt is not good for climbing. Macculloch says in his

Highlands and Isles of Scotland – 'To the north of [Gariveilan] it presents a long extended line of columnar cliffs; reaching in a gentle curve to 1000 yards or more, and impending, with its perpendicular face and broad mass of shadow, over the dark deep sea that washes its base. The height of this range varies from 300 to 400 ft.; and it thus forms one of the most magnificent colonnades to be found among the Western Islands. But these islands are nowhere more striking than when viewed at a sufficient distance from the northward; the whole of this lofty range of pillars being distinctly seen rising like a long wall out of the sea; varied by the ruder forms of the others which tower above or project beyond them, and contrasted by the wild rocks which skirt the whole group.'

Professor Heddle, who visited the island at the end of the last century, stated that the basaltic columns were 499 ft. in height.

Tom Weir says – 'The cliffs rise in great columns similar to the Giant's Causeway in Antrim and Fingal's Cave near Iona, but these are five times higher.

'To camp on Eilean an Tighe, with the hills of Harris in the background was like being on an inland sea, with islands on one side and mainland peaks on the other.' On this island a natural arch with good slabs above was climbed by T. Weir and I. Smart.

ROSS AND SUTHERLAND COAST

A number of small islands lie close to this coast or in various sea-lochs. Not many attain 300 ft.

The Summer Isles

Tanera More (406 ft.)
Maps: One-inch O.S., Seventh Series, sheet 19.
      Half-inch Bartholomew, sheet 58.

ACCESS:
Hire of boat to Summer Isles may be arranged with I. MacLeod, Achiltibuie Post Office. Tel 200.

The islands are of Torridonian sandstone and are nearly all

uninhabited except for Tanera More, where Dr. F. Fraser Darling worked a croft about which he wrote in *Island Farm*.

He describes Eilean a' Chleirich (Priest Island) in *Island Years*. It has two wild mammals apart from the grey seal, which are the pigmy shrew and the otter.

The climb from the south cave above the little boulder beach at Moll na h-Uamh to the summit cairn is steep. The view is very fine both to the east and west – the mainland and the Hebrides.

The island consists of two main masses cut by a glen running from south-west to north-east. The southern mass consisting of a ridge of Torridonian sandstone with cairn 252 ft. The northern face is steeper than the slope from the south cave, the strata having tilted to form rugged cliffs. It consists of fluted columns of great beauty, especially in the evening light.

At the south-eastern extremity there are two little corries, the floor of each being a flat peat bog. Two lochans cover part of the floor of the main glen, which are much frequented by otters. A patient observer, who is prepared to wait all night may be lucky enough to see the family on the grass in the early hours. The glen also divides the flora. Heather is dominant in the south, but in the north and west gives way to crowberry, sheeps fescue, buckthorn, plantain and thrift, bell heather and ling, bog asphodel and bog cotton.

Near Lochan Fada will be found aspen poplars growing to about 10 ft. high, flag irises, royal fern, honeysuckle and willow. Merganser breed along the banks.

On the south-east shore there is a cave, used in the past, for storing smuggled whisky. North of the east anchorage there are fine caves, and on the north side of the north-west point an interesting climb down the cliff to sea-level, where there is a long fissure leading through to the west side of the cliff.

HANDA

Sithein Mor (406 ft.)

Maps: One-inch O.S., Seventh Series, sheet 9.
Half-inch Bartholomew, sheet 58.

ACCESS:
Handa is a bird sanctuary and permission to visit the island should be

obtained from the Royal Society for the Protection of Birds, 21 Regent Terrace, Edinburgh.

A boat may be hired in Scourie from R. MacLeod, 6 Park Terrace. Telephone Scourie 40, or in Tarbet – a shorter crossing – from A. Munro, Tarbet Foindle, Telephone Scourie 26. The fare is approximately 30s. in each case.

The Great Stac of Handa

On 1st July, 1967, T. W. Patey, C. Bonington and I. McNaught-Davis made the second recorded crossing re-enacting the original exploit of nearly a century ago. Dr. Patey wrote:

'The Stac is 350 ft. high, cut vertically on every side, and lies on an inlet on the precipitous north side of the island of Handa. The enclosing walls are equally vertical or overhanging and the gap between the cliff-top and the flat summit of the Stac is 50 ft. at the narrowest point. We stretched 600 ft. of linked nylon ropes from side to side of the inlet so that the centre of our rope lay across the top of the Stac. To use the best anchorage points we had to cross the gap obliquely, so lengthening the Tyrolean traverse to 120 ft. Without the aid of Jumars it would have been difficult to overcome the considerable sag in the rope. Additional excitement was provided by numerous sea-birds cannoning into the taut nylon and by two guillemots on the Stac who started pecking the rope which had invaded their territory. The appalling 350 ft. chasm underneath made this a most impressive occasion.

'I found no traces of the earlier visit, although local reports confirm that the posts which were fixed on top of the Stac by the original visitor to provide a permanent rope anchorage, could still be seen up to 20 years ago. The pioneer traverse was certainly a remarkable 19th century exploit, perhaps more so than the feats on the St. Kilda crags. It is even more certain that no mountaineering amateur of that era would have committed himself to such an undertaking and possibly, despite modern equipment, many climbers will still find the traverse a thought-provoking experience.'

The exploit is recorded in Fauna of the North West Highlands (1904) by Harvie-Brown.

The Great Stac of Handa was climbed in 1963 by G. Hunter, D. Lang and H. MacInnes. The route they called the Great Arch was 380 ft. and Very Severe, and lies on the north face.

Overleaf: 21. Scuir of Eigg from Galmisdale.
Above: 22. Canna. Harbour and Compass Hill.
Below: 23. Shiants. Garbh Eilean from Eilean Mhuire.

Step off boat on to seaward side of Stac at steep green wall, piton in corner, and climb to ledge and belay (40 ft.). Climb wall right of belay to higher belay ledge. Follow steep groove to reach left traverse above the Great Arch overhangs. Continue traverse left (peg runner) into hidden corner, surmount wall and overhang above to piton belays on the Diving Board. 150 ft. of easier climbing follows to more broken rocks below the top. Scramble by loose chimney to summit. Descend by abseiling to Diving Board then by free abseil (dramatic) from a jammed nut to a boat aligned beneath. The rock is excellent and comparatively bird-free.

Stachan Geodh Bhrisidh which lies a quarter of a mile east of the Great Stac was climbed by a 200 ft. Very Severe route in 1969 by G. Hunter and D. Lang. The Stac which is really a huge flake which has slipped away from the main face is easily reached by descending steep grass from the cliff-top.

Start at arrow in corner on landward side. Traverse left to easier but loose rock leading to piton belay below a great corner crack. Climb corner using four pitons to belay on ledge with piled blocks (70 ft.). Climb flakes behind belay to crest to ridge, traverse right on rounded ledge on steep face for 30 ft. Follow first groove above to reach summit on knife edge. Descend the north-west face by abseiling from a bolt on summit to ledge 50 ft. below. A 150 ft. abseil from a chockstone reaches the base of the Stac.

AM BUACHAILLE

Maps: One-inch O.S., Seventh Series, sheet 9.
Half-inch, Bartholomew, sheet 58.

A handsome sharp pinnacle close to the shore between Sandwood Bay and Loch Inchard, within sight of Cape Wrath. T. Patey, J. Cleare and I. Clough who climbed it in 1967 said it was 200 ft. high and Very Severe.

Cross at low tide a 25 ft. channel using ladders or swimming (seaweed hazards) and fix 150 ft. Tyrolean rope. From low tide there is approximately four hours to complete the climb before the anchorage on shore becomes awash.

Start left of centre and climb overhanging rocks up and on to prow on right. Straight up till forced to traverse left. Left edge to ledge and rusty belay peg. Make awkward move from inset corner of ledge up and across retaining wall to ledge on right. Continue to 30 ft. crack. Climb – dubious rock – to other left traverse. Belay left edge (60 ft.). Move to deep overhanging crack. Traverse left below overhangs till possible to mantelshelf up between soup-plates. Cross slab to rejoin main crack. Pull out awkwardly at top (60 ft.).

CLETT ROCK, HOLBURN HEAD (160 ft.)

Maps: O.S. ND. 106 717.

This stac is separated from the mainland cliffs by an 80 ft. sea-channel. Although it would be possible to abseil down the mainland cliffs with a dinghy to paddle to the rock, this is not advisable because currents are dangerous. The local lobster fisher will put climbers on the rock and later collect. Heed should be paid to advice given by him about winds and tides as the spray is known to go over the top of the stac.

A severe A2 route has been done on the west face by R. Jolly, M. Willis and D. Young.

REFERENCES:

J. Macculloch, op. cit., Vol. iv (Small Isles). Vol. iii (Raasay, etc.).
Cruise of the Betsy, Hugh Miller.
Island Going, R. Atkinson, 1949. (Handa, Shiants).
Island Years and *Island Farm,* F. Fraser Darling.
Scottish Mountaineering Club Journal –
   Vol. 29, p. 54. Eigg, by Ian Clough.
Yorkshire Rambler's Club Journal, Vol. 5, p. 34. Eigg, by M. Botterill.

6

The Long Island (Outer Hebrides)

The Long Island, which forms the greater part of the Outer Hebrides, is the great chain of islands stretching 130 miles from Barra Head in the south to the Butt of Lewis in the north. They are separated from Skye by the Little Minch, 15 miles at its narrowest. The principal islands in the chain are:

> North Lewis (Stornoway, Park and Uig)
> West Harris and West Lewis.
> Harris (south, including Tarbert).
> North Uist (north part) including most of the South of Harris.
> Eriskay, South Uist, Benbecula, North Uist, Monach Isles.
> Barra Head or Berneray, Mingulay, Sandray, Pabbay, Vatersay and Barra.

As the northernmost isles are the most important from the point of view of climbing and access, they are dealt with first.

NORTH LEWIS

Ben Barvas (955 ft.), 5 miles north-west of Stornoway.

Maps: One-inch O.S., Seventh Series, sheet 8.
      Half-inch Bartholomew, sheet 57.

ACCESS:
MacBraynes steamers run from Mallaig to Stornoway. The shortest and quickest sea crossing is by car ferry from Uig in Skye to Tarbert, Harris, and thence by road to Stornoway. There is an air service to Stornoway.

To the climber the northern part of Lewis has little attraction, with low, rounded hills of which Ben Barvas is the highest. At the Butt of Lewis, a rugged headland, there are cliffs 75 to 100 ft. high.

A few climbs have been done on the cliffs and stacks near the light-house. At the north end of the island, one mile south-west of the Butt of Lewis, is Pigmies Isle (Luchruban), separated from the main-land by a deep cleft. A chambered building stands on the summit, to which the climb is perilous.

The standing stones at Callernish, 15 miles west from Stornoway, near the head of Loch Roag, are worth a visit. They are next in importance to Stonehenge.

The magnificent morse (walrus tusk) chessmen, dating from the tenth and twelfth centuries were found here. Some are in the Museum of Antiquities, Edinburgh, and some in London.

Dun Carloway, on the west coast is one of the best preserved brochs in Scotland. The wall is 10 ft. thick at the base, and at one point rises to a height of 30 ft.

PARK (LEWIS)

Feirihisval (1074 ft.).   Map reference 302146.   1 mile S.S.E. of head of
                  Loch Seaforth, and 2 miles E.N.E. of
Mor Monadh (1314 ft.).   1 mile East of
Sithean an Ai-rgid (1250 ft.).   1½ miles N.N.W. of
Muaithabhal (1386 ft.).   1¼ miles West of
Beinn na h-Uamha (1197 ft.).   2 miles North-East of
Beinn Mhor (1847 ft.).   1 mile N.N.E. of
Carn Ban (1571 ft.).   3 miles N.N.E. of
Caiteshal (1473 ft.).
Maps: One-inch O.S., Seventh Series, sheet 18.
      Half-inch Bartholomew, sheet 57.

ACCESS:
This area of very hilly country east of Loch Seaforth is difficult of access. A track which leaves the Tarbet–Stornoway road half a mile south of the bridge over Auchuinn Mhor (map reference 262193), if followed for 4 miles, leads to within 1½ miles of Feirihisval. Otherwise a canoe or folding boat in which to cross Loch Seaforth seems the only solution.

There is no accommodation in the area.

The cliffs below Caiteshal look worth investigating. Otherwise there do not appear to be other features on the hills in the district of interest to climbers.

UIG (Lewis)

Mealisval (1885 ft.)
Cracaval (1682 ft.)
Tarain (1347 ft.)
Tahaval (1688 ft.)
Teinnasval (1626 ft.)
Tamanaisval – Creag Dubh Dhibadail (1530 ft.)

Maps: One-inch O.S., Seventh Series, sheet 12.
Half-inch Bartholomew, sheet 57.

ACCESS:

It may be advisable to hire a car at Stornoway. There is from time to time a bus to Islivig, but it is not to be depended on, though a car hirer in Uig may meet the bus at Garynahine. Enquiries should be made locally. Uig is 35 miles from Stornoway, 21 from Garynahine.

ACCOMMODATION:

There are no hotels, but one can usually arrange to be put up in one of the houses at Ardroil. In selecting a campsite, shelter from the prevailing wind is often as crucial a consideration as the state of the ground. The present writer remembers the bus-driver who abandoned his vehicle – and passengers – for half an hour to see that he found a good site.

Uig is a delightful place with fine coastal scenery. The white sands of Uig Bay and Mangersta Bay are superb, and the rocky coast between worth visiting, especially when a big sea is coming in from the Atlantic. North of Uig Bay the coast is rocky and to the east of Gallan Head are some high cliffs.

Glen Valtos, through which the road to Uig passes after leaving Loch Roag is a narrow defile, $1\frac{1}{2}$ miles in length, with steep rocks on both sides. At the deepest part the gorge is 400 ft. wide with 250 ft. faces on either side.

Mealisval (1885 ft.) at the northern end of the west group about 3 miles south of Uig Bay. The north and east slopes are steep and rocky, whilst that to the west is easy and offers interesting climbing. Mula Mac Sgiathain, the north-eastern shoulder, has a steep precipice on its northern face overlooking Loch Mor na Clibhe. It is about

1000 ft. high and is called Creagan Thealastail. The face is cleft, for its full height, by a central gully – **Palla Glas**. There are two fissures, the main one, and another to its left, at a slightly higher altitude. The main gully is continuous with three pitches half-way up, which do not appear to have been climbed. The secondary gully is not so continuous. The middle section, however, is very definite and has a pitch which can be circumvented by a ridge on the right with a crack above which might afford a good line of ascent. Near the foot of the secondary chimney is a grassy terrace on which it is possible to traverse and, by way of a vegetatious chimney gain the easy buttress to the east.

This buttress consists of slabs of clean rock at an easy angle. Keeping to the right gives an interesting scramble with a 12 ft. pitch about 300 ft. up. To the right of Palla Glas is a fine ridge with a chimney at the top. The vegetation is luxuriant. Further to the right on the face are three shallow chimneys.

A route giving 700 ft. of 'Difficult' climbing was made by Folkard and party in 1948. The rock in the lower section is smooth, but becomes rougher above. It starts in the centre of the buttress to the left of a black section of rock (cairn). A feature of the climb is a small pinnacle just beyond a large area of overhanging black rock (cairn), and a vertical wall above, which is climbed to the right.

The buttress to the left seems easier, and that to the right, harder. There are steep crags on the east side of Mealisval overlooking the glen.

The easiest way of ascent is up the west slope from the coast road, about 3 miles south of Ardroil. The east side may be easily climbed by a steep slope to the left of the eastern buttress from near the foot of Loch Raonasgail.

The Flannan Isles 22 miles, and St. Kilda 60 miles away, can be seen from the summit.

Cracaval (1682 ft.). From Mealisval a stony slope reminiscent of the Cairngorms, leads south to a rocky bealach (975 ft.) with three lochans, beyond which an easy broken up ridge leads to the summit of Cracaval. The east face is steep and rocky, but would probably not afford any rock-climbing.

South of Cracaval, south-east over the Bealach Raonasgail (850 ft.) are the two Liavals (1625 ft. and 1645 ft.) which have a steep eastern side. Three miles south of Mealisval is **Griomaval** (1625 ft.) which has an 800 ft. face on the side overlooking the Dubh Loch. The east shoulder is easy. This mountain is probably the best view-point in Uig. The easiest way to reach it is probably by road to Meal-ista, then either up the west slope, or by Glen Tealasdale, Dubh Loch and the east slope which is more interesting.

In June 1969 R. Sharp and W. Sproul made an 800 ft. Severe route on the Tealasdale slabs of Griomaval which they called *Islivig Direct*. It takes a direct line from the tail of the lowest slabs to the summit of Griomaval following a crack and corner system.

On the same face they also did a grassy rake which separates the right-hand buttress from the main slab. It was 800 ft. and Difficult, and was named *Golden Gully*.

An interesting alternative route back to Ardroil is from the top of North Liaval to descend to the Bealach Raonasgail, from which a rough path leads northwards to Loch Mor na Clibhe. From here the direct route to Ardroil by the stream is somewhat wet and soft. A drier route is to skirt the foot of Mula Mac Sgiathain, then strike due north for the east side of Loch na Faoirbh and finally by a peat road to the coast road.

Tarain (1346 ft.) – is the highest point in the interesting country called Eadan Dha Fhaoghail, forming the northern end of the eastern group of Uig hills. There is a great deal of rock exposed in this area and a number of lochans in the hollows of the hills. The north face of Tarain offers rock climbing.

1½ miles north of Tarain, immediately to the west of Loch Suinaval are two rock summits – **Beannan a Tuath** (755 ft.) and **Beannan a Deas** (825 ft.). They consist of good clean rock and rise up steeply from the moor. On the north-west side of the latter is a steep, slabby face which along with the north face provide routes of all degrees of difficulty. These little hills are about 2 miles from Ardroil.

Tahaval (1688 ft.) rises fairly steeply opposite the south end of Loch Raonasgail. Though highest it is probably the least interesting of the eastern group.

Teinnasval (1625 ft.) which is the next peak to the south is similar physically, except for its western face which is steep and much more interesting. It is called – *Sgoran Dubh Theinneasbhal*. The face is split into two parts by a stone shoot, which forks half-way up. The following nomenclature is suggested:

The buttress left of the main forked gully, *North Buttress*; that between the two branches of the fork, *Central Buttress*; that to the right, *South Buttress*; and the buttress south of the three parallel gullies, *Far South Buttress*; the three gullies, *Nos. 1, 2* and *3 gullies* respectively, No. 1 being nearest to *Far South Buttress*.

North Buttress. Broken rock. Might give a certain amount of scrambling.

Central Buttress. The lower part looks impracticable and the upper an easy scramble.

South Buttress. Steep, and cut into by four narrow chimneys. From a point a short distance up the main forked gully rises a very steep and deeply cut incision, containing numerous pitches. On the right of this is a fine buttress after which the face is cut into by three parallel chimneys.

South Buttress (490 ft.), was climbed in 1948 by Folkard and Wills. Start at the lowest part of the main buttress overlooking the main gully (cairn). The first pitch of 20 ft. is up the steep rib to a grass platform, then traverse left on to a triangular rock projecting over the gully. About half-way up there is a huge overlapping slab, like a tile on a roof, which blocks the way except to the right. Climb it a few feet from its right-hand edge to half-way up, then traverse left and surmount overlap by a delicate move and continue upwards to a fine stance behind a pile of rocks. Traverse left below the final overhang until a small bulge is reached; this is surmounted on good holds to easier rocks which are ascended till it is possible to scramble on to the roof of the overhang (cairn).

Far South Buttress (440 ft., Very Difficult). The lowest portion of the buttress can be avoided by walking on to a grassy shelf from the right. Start just left of and a little above the lowest point of the lower section of the buttress (cairn).

Three short pitches give 85 ft. of moderate climbing to the grassy shelf, this is followed by 90 ft. of scrambling to the foot of a large

24. *Overleaf:* Handa.

25. *Above:* The Butt of Lewis.

26. The North Lewis hills across Loch Resort.

27. *Above left:* Lewis. Far South Buttress, Sgoran Dubh Theinneasbhal.
28. *Below left:* Creag Dubh Dhibadail.

29. North Rona, the summit.

30. Strone Ulladale. D. Scott on first ascent of The Scoop.

31. Harris. Lochan a Ghlinn region from Scarp.

32. Harris. Uisgnaval More, Mulla Fodheas and Clisham.

slab lowest at its right end. Climb 35 ft. and traverse left to reach the foot of a black groove. After another 200 ft. of climbing, a slab of superb roughness is reached, leading to a stance and belay just left of a small overhang. Climb small crack on right and up slab (30 ft.).

The Three Gullies. Nos. 1 and 3 are well-defined for most of their height. No. 2 is hardly a gully at all when seen close up.

No. 1 Rib lies between Nos. 1 and 2 gullies (445 ft., Very Difficult). The start is at a tongue of rock coming down from rib into No. 2 Gully (cairn). Rather more than half-way up is a nose above which the holds virtually disappear, but the angle soon eases. (Leader in socks on this pitch, would be at least severe in boots.)

The rib between No. 3 Gully and the South Buttress should give a good climb.

Tamanaisval – Creag Dubh Dhibadail

Tamanaisval (1530 ft.) lies to the south-east of the bealach from the last two summits. On its south side, overlooking Loch Dibadale is a cliff half a mile long and over 400 ft. high. The average angle of the central section is about 85 degrees and the rock is said to be of a smoother texture than that of other faces nearby. Two routes have been reported on this face – the most impressive on the island after Sgurr Ulladale. To the left – the south side – a 600 ft. route was climbed by W. Sproul and R. Sharp up slabs and crack-lines. Picking the easiest line 'where the rocks are not so steep' they found it fairly difficult.

Suainaval (1404 ft.) is the most north-eastern of the Uig group of hills two miles from the south-east corner of Uig Bay. It has a steep rocky face overlooking Loch Suainaval, and there is a small steep low lying hill, Sron ri Gaoith, one mile to the south of it.

NORTH HARRIS

Clisham (2622 ft.)
Gillaval Glas (1544 ft.) and
Sgaoth Ard (1829 ft.)

Toddun (1731 ft.)
Uisgnaval More (2393 ft.)
Oreval (2165 ft.) and
Ullsval (2153 ft.)
Tirga More (2227 ft.)

Maps: One-inch O.S., Seventh Series, sheet 12.
Half-inch Bartholomew, sheet 57.

ACCESS:
With the new ferry service making the short crossing from Uig in
Skye, and the excellent road up to and through that island, the
access to Tarbert, Harris, has been improved as much as was Glencoe
by the new road.

These ferries operate on weekdays as do the flights from Abbotsinch (Glasgow). There are several buses through the day between
Stornoway and Tarbert, and on Mondays, Wednesdays and Fridays
between Huishnish and Tarbert.

ACCOMMODATION:
Tarbert Hotel at the head of East Loch Tarbert offers full board.
A hostel at Rainigadale (by Tarbert) is run by the Gatliffe Trust.
There are many private houses offering bed and breakfast. It is
difficult to find campsites that are not boggy and midge-infested in
summer.

Clisham (2622 ft.) is the highest summit in the Outer Hebrides. It is
5 miles due north from Tarbert. It is a well-defined peak from the
south-east and from south-west shows an open corrie of broken-up
tiers of rock, Coire Dubh, backed by the summit ridge running from
the highest top to the small peak of Ant-Isean and the west peak,
Mulla-fo-dheas. The Tarbert–Stornoway road gives convenient
access to the eastern slopes of the hill either by Loch a Mhorghain
or Sgurr Scaladle, up Glen Scaladale. The south-east slopes are all
quite easy. The final summit ridge is just broad enough to hold the
Ordnance Survey cairn. The north-east slope is steep and fringed
with crags at the top.

The main ridge west is a stony slope down to the Bealach (1080 ft.)
then ascends easily to Ant-Isean (2280 ft.), a small grassy top from
which slabby rocks slope down into Coire Dubh. Beyond Ant-
Isean the ridge narrows, and after a dip (*c.* 2190 ft.) rises up steeply

over good rock, which gives an interesting, short climb to the west summit Mulla-fo-thuath (2360 ft.). It is a fine summit with some interesting crags, on which it is well worth spending some time and energy, on its western side. The south-western corrie with 'jagged outline' perpendicular walls, and semi-craterlike aspect' has been mentioned.

It is easier to recross Mulla-fo-dheas and descend by its south-west shoulder towards the derelict whaling station at the head of Loch Bun Abhainn-eadar than to descend to the glen to the west-ward, Abhainn Loch a' Sgail, where the going is rough.

Seton Gordon found Clisham and its environment singularly devoid of bird and animal life compared with, say the Cairngorms. He found grouse and meadow pipits, but no curlew or golden plover; even buzzards, numerous in Mull, seemed absent. The eagle was formerly found here. There is scarcely any heather on the hill; but wild thyme was found everywhere even at the summit, along with saxifrages and violets. Nearby were a few alpine willow and rose-root but the delicate flowers of silene acaulis and azales procumbens were lacking – the latter an essentially granite-loving plant.

In *A Highland Year* the same author said that rabbits were once very numerous on the driest slopes of Clisham. Ferrets, which also preyed on the ptarmigan, are, in his opinion responsible for their extermination. So this animal achieved what the related pine marten failed to do in the forest of Harris. (The forest here means a wild expanse. There are no trees at all in the stony wilderness.)

The northern ends of the spurs jutting into Glen Scaladale and Langadale – the latter running more north and south – are the features of the Clisham massif most likely to interest the rock-climber.

Sgurr Scaladale has a face on the north-east side which is about half a mile in length. It is crossed diagonally by a broad grass ledge which begins at the foot of the face at the east end and rises to the summit of the crag at the west end. There are three gullies, the east one starting at the beginning of the grass traverse. The centre one was climbed by Botterill and party. It started at 535 ft. and gave no difficulty till the grass traverse. At the penultimate pitch the party had to traverse out on to the western buttress. The total climb was about 775 ft. M. K. and N. S. Tennent climbed the central rib in

1954. The face was steep and though the holds were small the rock was sound and clean. The final pitch was a crack with inside walls of glassy rock crystals into which hands had to be jammed. M. K. emerged from the top like Lady Macbeth from Duncan's bedchamber.

Miolnir 465 ft. Very Severe. R. B. Evans, L. A. Howarth and Mrs. Evans.

The obvious feature of the main crag, left of the central gully, is a steep black wall with a dark cleft towards the left – a gully developing into an overhanging groove. The climb takes the lower part of the cleft and then breaks out left to ascend a deep V-groove. A very fine steep route.

Gain the gully after 100 ft. of slabs on the left. Follow gully for 80 ft. Go up groove on right, then back into a chimney to a boulder-strewn platform; piton belay on smaller ledge left 15 ft. Climb steep wall to below overhang; peg runner. Move right and up deep groove to ledge on left. With peg aid pull over the overhang and go left to stance and peg belay (100 ft.). Traverse right into groove; go up to slabs and peg belay. Finish up steep corner above.

West Buttress (750 ft. Very Severe), was done by A. Powling and D. Yates in 1959. The climb takes a direct line up the obvious buttress right of the main crag, just left of a gully. Start at the lowest rocks.

Grassily up leftwards, then back rightwards to stance and pinnacle (120 ft.). Straight up over rock and grass to stance below small overhang (120 ft.). Break out rightwards, then go up to small stance beneath long crack (60 ft.). Up crack for 40 ft., then right to thin crack very near right edge of buttress. Up this, step left and climb face for 30 ft. to grass stance (100 ft.). Go up rock above – then a greasy crack (crux) to another grass stance (50 ft.). Scrambling to top (300 ft.) – possibly Duncan's bedchamber.

Cnoc a Chaisteil at the north end of the spur running north from Mulla-fo-thuath through Mullach an Langa is a rock face 200/300 ft. high. It was climbed at its western end up a rib consisting of square cut blocks, leading to sloping platform and notched block (loose) at top. To the left the face is steeper and less broken.

Creag Mo, Glen Scaladale, is a rock face to the north of the stream, running north and south, where two routes were done in 1955.

Gollum (340 ft., Severe). Start near the far right end of the wall to the right of the central overhanging amphitheatre at an obvious easy-angled slabby rib (cairn). Climb rib and steep groove to ledge, left. Trend right over slab, overlap and up a steep little wall to a stance, left, on large detached blocks (100 ft.). Climb slab and short groove above to grassy rake. Go on to wall above some large blocks at an obvious left traverse, then go right to a large grassy bay. Walk 30 ft. left to a prominent cracked corner (120 ft.). Climb corner to the top (120 ft.).

M. A. and B. Reeves did a 320 ft. Hard Severe route – *Smeagol* – leading directly to the 'cracked corner'. It starts a few yards left of the start of the above, on the clean right edge of a vegetated recess.

Miny (350 ft., Severe), is to the right of the overhanging central amphitheatre where the wall is broken half-way by a short grass terrace, easily accessible. The start is at the left-hand side of the lower wall. Go up slabs past a small sapling to grass terrace. From right of the terrace a steep groove leads to the top. First ascent by Evans, Howarth and Evans.

Note: The route *Miny* appears to share at least the same finish with *Gollum*.

Herbivore (340 ft., Very Severe), was climbed by P. T. Newall and C. G. Winfield in summer 1969.

About 100 ft. left of the amphitheatre is a long overhang low down. Right of this is a short slab at the foot of the face.

Climb right edge of slab to grassy niche below small overhang. Step left and take this at obvious weakness. Continue right up grass and rock to base of corner. Piton belay (100 ft.). Move round bulge to ledge on right. Up corner using thin flake to small ledge on left wall. Tend left to larger ledge below corner. Small nuts and pitons and belays (60 ft.). Climb corner for about 15 ft., traverse right to shallow depression, descend about 6 ft. and traverse small sloping ledge round arête on right to small grass platform and jammed flake belay at base of corner (35 ft.). Climb leaning corner and exit right over heather to small nut and spike belays (25 ft.). Swing up left on to slab, cross this to corner and ascend scoop on left wall to ledge. Go left and up short corner to finish up steep vegetation (120 ft.).

Gillaval Glas (1544 ft.) and **Sgaoth Ard** (1829 ft.), which lie immediately north of Tarbert, may be climbed from there in a short day. Along with Sgaoth Iosal (1740 ft.) they form a horseshoe around the east end of Glen Skeaudale. The southern slopes consist of glaciated rocks interspersed with grass and a profusion of perched blocks. To the east the hills descend steeply into Glen Laxadale with two fine crags, Creag na h-Iolaire and Sron an Toister. The northern face of Gillival Glas, especially its western end, Cnoc Eadar Da Bheinn, is precipitous and cut by several gullies.

No. 1 Buttress – Hauds (234 ft., Very Severe). H. Small and J. W. Graham.

Start in steep narrow gully right of nose, below steep groove in left wall (cairn). Climb groove (peg runner) to belay on top of pinnacle (60 ft.). Climb the steep wall above to block belay (70 ft.). Scramble up easier rock going right to a small pinnacle overlooking the gully (114 ft.).

Variation Finish, which is severe, was done by I. G. Rowe and P. MacDonald in 1969. From the top of the pinnacle, traverse right for 20 ft. and climb the edge of the buttress.

Toddun (1731 ft.), is the highest hill between Loch Seaforth and Glen Laxadale. If its ascent is included in a round trip from Tarbert, it involves nearly 4000 ft. of climbing – an interesting excursion. The Kyles–Scalpay road is followed to the outlet from Loch Laxadale, from which a good bridle-path rises to cross the north shoulder of Beinn a'Chaolais at a height of 950 ft. The track then zig-zags steeply down to the picturesque Loch Trollamarig, rises again to another height, then to Gary-aloteger, from where the ascent of Toddun may be made by the south-east slope and ridge. The summit has a fine view of Loch Seaforth. Return by the west slope, keeping well north to avoid steep rocks, and over An Reithe (1400 ft.) to the footbridge at the outlet from upper Loch Laxadale. An old grass-grown road on the west side of Glen Laxadale leads over the bealach (450 ft.) at the head of the glen, and joins the main road beyond the Maaruig river.

Uisgnaval More (2392 ft.), is the highest of the line of hills west of the Clisham group, and is bounded on the west by Glen Meavaig.

From the south, it, and Toilesval (2272 ft.) immediately to the north, show up as fine pointed summits. Uisgnaval More throws out a long shoulder to the north-west which terminates in Strone Scourst (1608 ft.), an impressive rockly bluff overlooking the head of Loch Scourst. M. Slesser and D. Bennet did a 300 ft. route here which they rated as Mild Severe. A direct line was taken up the west end. Under the steepest part of the cliff an old fence ends at a smooth vertical wall. Start a few yards north of fence up more broken rocks with a rightward traverse to a vertical chimney. Go up this for 15 ft. then traverse right to exposed ledge. Climb more or less directly up steep rocks to broad ledge 150 ft. above start. Continue slightly rightwards to short awkward groove.

The west face of the Strone is composed of rock faces and terraces, and apart from the line just mentioned there are few that appear to give continuous routes. Indefinite routes have been done on the north-west face and the gully system on the north has been used for descent several times.

Craig Stulaval (1684 ft.), is at the north end of the group, over-looking Loch Stulsdale. The extensive crags to its north should repay investigation.

Uisgnaval More and the rest of the group present no difficulties from the south. There is a good road in the west side for about five miles for the use of the fishing tenants. The proprietor tends to be discouraging, and keeps the gate at the main road locked.

Oreval (2165 ft.) and **Ullaval** (2153 ft.), are the highest summits in the group of Harris hills between Glen Meavaig and Gleann Chliostair running north from West Loch Tarbert to the head of Loch Resort, a distance of eight miles. Oreval has a steep rocky face overlooking Glen Caadale Ear and Loch Scourst. The northern end of Ullaval is the great overhanging cliff of Strone Ulladale, which along with Corrievreckan, the vast cliffs of St. Kilda and perhaps a few others, must be one of the most awesome features in the islands. The nose, rising to 1205 ft. above the loch in one bold sweep, is Britain's largest overhang.

Strone Ulladale. The best approach to Strone Ulladale is from

Tarbert to Amhuinnsuidhe (bus to Huishnish twice a week) and then by a good path through Gleann Chliostair to Loch Ulladale. The shorter approach from Loch Resort is rough and boggy; up the river Housay is better from Kinloch Resort. There is also a private road up Glen Meavaig to Lochan an Fheoir from where the Strone can be easily reached over the shoulder to the west.

To the left of the nose as seen from the Loch is the East Wall; on its right is the massive West Wall running south for half a mile to the South Buttress with its diagonal gangway. This 800 ft. wall is seamed with grooves, topped by overhangs.

The rock is a very solid grey gneiss.

East Wall is divided by two huge gullies, Great Gully on the left, which cleaves the whole height of the face, and the Recess. This part of the face is known as the Amphitheatre, the floor of which consists of a large grassy platform cut off from below by heavily vegetated rock faces. Two grassy rakes extend to the left from the Amphitheatre, starting below the buttress, dividing the Amphitheatre from the Great Gully (Amphitheatre Buttress). One of these rises as far as the Great Gully, where it peters out. The other consists of a steep grassy rake immediately below the left base of Amphitheatre Buttress, and continues as far as Great Gully, where there is an easy crossing (approach to Solari's and Iren's climb; the first recorded on this face). To the right of the Amphitheatre and just above the grass slopes below it is a small rush-covered shelf (Rush Shelf) immediately below the Great Overhang.

Great Gully itself is a disappointing climb, with more grass than rock. It gives approximately 1000 ft. of climbing. Evil-looking pitches are avoided on the left. The crux – a square amphitheatre one-third of the way up – is unavoidable and is climbed in two pitches. The first, 40 ft., goes up a leftward-slanting groove; the second, 90 ft., traverse right and up a groove through an overhang (Very Severe).

The buttress to the left of Great Gully has been climbed starting a few feet left of the gully where there is a lot of vegetation, the first 150 ft. being up steep heather to a rowan tree. Good rock is gained above a second rowan to the right. Up slabs moving right and over a bulge to small stance and piton belay below an overhang. Traverse right below the bulge, then climb easier rock overlooking the gully to a platform and peg belay below a steep groove. This is climbed with a peg belay on ledge on right (60 ft.) to a terrace. 200 ft. of pleasant slabs lead to the top.

This route which is 630 ft. and severe, and the previous one, was climbed in 1961 by Evans, Howarth and Evans. Another approach – in from the left – to this very good line was made by I. Rowe and P. Macdonald straight up the centre of the buttress, using a leftward slanting groove.

Climb steep and dangerous grass to reach the rock (200 ft.). Climb to tree on ledge, move left and climb short, strenuous crack system to eyrie below overhang fault (100 ft.). Move down and right into the fault and climb it leftwards to large ledge (8 pegs and nuts,

Fig. 4 STRONE ULLADALE *South-East Face*

R – Recess   RP – Rush Platform   GG – Great Gully

1. No. 1 Buttress
2. Solari and Iren's Route
3. No. 3 Buttress
4. Amphitheatre Arête
5. Inversion
6. Evans Howarth and Evans Route
7. The Iron Butterfly
8. The Scoop

110 ft.). Move left to surmount bulge (peg) on to slab, then rightwards into corner, which climb to belay (120 ft.). Easier rocks lead to the summit.

The route, which is 900 ft. in total, is Very Severe, and A2, was climbed in May 1969 and named *Iron Butterfly*.

To the left of the upper half of Great Gully are three routes on buttresses or ribs starting at about the level of the Amphitheatre. They are numbered from right to left, No. 2 being the original route done by Solari and Iren in July 1938. The description of their climb is as follows: Easy slabs to amphitheatre at foot of great recess. (There are various ways up the lower crag and the description of some have been published. It tends to be too indeterminate, broken and vegetatious to merit detailed accounts. It is easier on the whole, slanting in from the right, whence Rush Platform is easily gained.) Cross the great gully leftwards by steep grass to buttress divided by two chimneys. Climb the right chimney till a severe traverse can be made to a prominent rib. The rib is climbed on good holds until a traverse can be made across the left-hand chimney to another rib. The buttress above provides exposed but not difficult climbing on sound, clean rock – 600 ft. Very Difficult.

No. 1 Buttress (between two branches of Great Gully above the easy upper grass crossing) – 250 ft., Difficult. Start in the lesser branch gully to the left of the buttress and a few feet above its base. A direct start could not be made and a short traverse was made into a groove on the left, leading to a grass slope above the overhang (70 ft.). Traverse right on to buttress at some large blocks, thence to the top (180 ft. of climbing, then scrambling).

No. 3 Buttress (numbered from the right) – Difficult. The lower grass slopes are followed to Great Gully (entered by an airy ledge). A grassy rake passes round the foot of No. 2 Buttress and the start is made on the left of No. 3 Buttress (cairn). This gives a somewhat artificial route with 145 ft. of climbing followed by 120 ft. of scrambling.

Amphitheatre Buttress is between the Great Gully and the Recess. Start at foot of buttress (cairn) – 465 ft., Severe. Follow grass rake for 30 ft. till lodgement can be made on buttress. Ascending traverse left to small cave 70 ft. (poor stance and belay). Traverse right and climb wall to grass ledge (50 ft.). Climb slab to heather ledge (50 ft.). A 40-ft. wall is climbed first leftward, then rightward to heather ledge. The wall above climbed to left to below overhang, which was passed to the right first on rock, then steep moss. The rock regained, continue to good stance overlooking Great Gully (100 ft.). The rib above leads to a commodious platform with huge boulder at back and overlooks Great Gully. Climb wall on right, then slab followed by a small holdless rib (40 ft.). 40 ft. of scrambling leads to a good stance (cairn). There is probably quite a lot of variation possible on this route. On the first ascent the leader did the last pitch minus a boot and combined tactics were used.

To the right of Amphitheatre Buttress is the Recess, and to the right again, on the face between it and the Nose there is a fine route, *Inversion*. This route was the first to attack seriously the challenge of the Strone. It keeps close to the left of the Nose and goes over several roofs free of aid. It was climbed in August 1965 by M. A. Reeves and J. Ball, is 580 ft. and Very Severe.

Start from the Rush Platform. Before the Recess the upper buttress degenerates into steep vegetation, but directly above is a clean, steep face. Start in the centre of this (cairn).

Go up steep rocks and then a shallow groove until possible to go right beneath a large overhang to a vertical black groove. Climb this, then a short rib on the right to a good ledge beneath the first great overhanging barrier (80 ft.) chockstone belay. Traverse right beneath the roof to a cracked overhanging weakness on the edge. Climb this on surprising holds then a further 20 ft. to a small stance (40 ft.). The second barrier of overhangs is now above. Traverse left round corner to overhanging groove. Climb this (Difficult) to a roof, step down left then reach over roof to a hidden edge. Mantelshelf up to slanting niche, then right (awkward) to an easier wall above. Climb wall to stance level with an obvious right traversing line (70 ft.). Traverse down to right, then up to the edge at about 40 ft., climb the bulge above to the left of a chimney (loose blocks), then trend left to small ledge on the nose (awkward). Go straight up slab for 15 ft. then diagonally right to large triangular greasy stance (90 ft.). Peg belay. Climb up the broad ledge above, going slightly right on slabby rock to shallow black groove. Go up left then back right up short grassy rake to a belay beneath very steep rock (120 ft.). Go left on to a large block then up steep nose to easier ground (80 ft.). Easy rocks lead to the top (100 ft.).

North-West Face Direct (The Scoop). Grade A4, Very Severe, 560 ft., 90 pegs, 1 bolt, 5 pitches. 30 hours of climbing.

Start: Climb up slabs at the bottom of the face for 150 ft. to an earth ledge about 50 ft. below a rush platform.

1. 130 ft. (A2). Step down a few feet from the belay and climb up to an overhang. Place a peg on the left and pull over the overhang to place another peg. Step up and with a sling round a flake on the right reach a shallow bay. Now move right, ascending with the aid of pegs and difficult free moves in between. Begin to peg directly up overhanging rock when under the general line. Reach a ledge of loose blocks and belay.

2. 50 ft. (A2). Step up right and surmount loose overhead flakes. Step over them with care to reach a shallow corner. Peg up this to a good ledge on left.

3. 130 ft. (A3). Step left from the ledge and ascend loose flakes for a few feet to reach a solid corner above. The rock bulges then relent to the vertical below a square cut overhang. Surmount this on the left and overcome a band of mica schist. Climb loose blocks to a corner of red quartz. Climb to a further and bigger block overhang. Peg out under to the left. Continue pegging to the next roof and make a spectacular pendule out left to another good belay ledge 5 ft. below.

4. 100 ft. (A4). Tension back to the corner and climb back up to the roof. Again, turn the block on the left, with 'chocks' and 'bongs' lightly used, owing to the apparent detached nature of the block. Peg up to a smaller block overhang then reach round horizontally right 6 ft., and climb up until the narrow crack peters out. Use a bolt, *in situ*, and place a peg high up on the right. Follow this line over the last overhang until one can look up the final pitch, now vertical. Reach a sloping slab on the right and belay.

5. 150 ft. (A1, H.V.S.). Climb up right and follow a thin crack up a brown wet streak on the wall with pegs and very severe free moves. Continue more easily over sloping blocks to the end of the climb. Scrambling leads to the top.

This route was made between 31st May and 5th June, 1969, by D. Scott, J. Upton, G. Lee and M. Terry. It goes to the left of a route up the central groove done by K. Spence and J. Porteus in June 1969.

The Right Wall (West Wall). The long line of cliff bounding Upper Glen Ulladale on its east, from the Great Nose of the Strone to an easier-angled buttress – South Buttress – which is split by an obvious gangway. The main right wall of Strone Ulladale appears to offer plenty of scope, but holds are almost entirely lacking. The most feasible major route seems to be *Midgard*, which takes a snaking traverse along an obvious weakness. *Gangway*, Difficult, takes the obvious gangway which splits South Buttress from left to right. Reach the gangway by a steep corner and short traverse left followed by 200 ft. of pleasant slabs, then scrambling.

Midgard starts about 80 ft. left of the *Gangway* at the lowest point of a tongue of rock – *c.* 600 ft., Very Difficult. A good route with exposed situations, it takes the easiest line up the wall.

Go up slabby rock on left to bank of yellow rock. Move right along ledge to a belay (60 ft.). Move up to right for 20 ft., then left a few feet, traverse right again to belay below an overhang (70 ft.), at the obvious traverse line, which follow left into a corner. Then go up slab and grass patch to a small flake belay after 100 ft. Continue the traverse to base of the second grass patch. Move down a little and across to an easy gangway which leads to the top. Peg belays used.

Apart from the Nose itself the most direct line on the West Face to date is *Stone*. 700 ft. Very Severe and A2. Climbed by J. Porteus and K. Spence on 22nd and 23rd May, 1969.

Starting from the lowest point of the main face, this route makes for the quartz ramp and twin-crack corner splitting the upper part of the face.

Climb corner to large flake (80 ft.). Descend rightwards and traverse beneath overlaps for 100 ft., then up through break to belay (110 ft.). Traverse back left, then go up to small roof. Turn this on left (peg) and belay on right (45 ft.). Traverse left 20 ft. to quartz corner and climb this (pegs) to Ramp (45 ft.). Follow the Ramp to the foot of the corner. Belay on grass ledge (100 ft.). Climb left-hand crack, traverse into right-hand crack below roof and continue to turf (pegs). Belay on grass ledge above (140 ft.). Go up corner (pegs) for 30 ft. and traverse right round corner to belay (50 ft.). Finish up easier rocks (120 ft.).

Prelude, 600 ft., Mild Severe. M. A. Reeves and J. Grieve, 1967.

A good route which starts in the same general weakness as Midgard (q.v.) crossing this and taking a direct line up the wall. Start on West Wall, just left of light-coloured tongue of rock 100 ft. left of South Buttress gangway. Climb obvious cracked groove left of pillar then up rightwards to ledges (120 ft.). Right up a few feet then back left up a

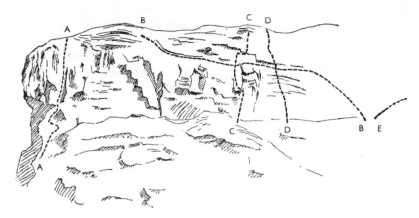

Fig. 5   STRONE ULLADALE   *The Right (West) Wall*

A – Stone   C – Aurora   E – The Gangway
B – Midgard   D – Prelude

sort of gangway to weakness in bulges above. Step up and traverse about 30 ft. horizontally right by smooth sloping ledge to easy groove. Up this and bear left on slabs (120 ft.). Go straight up with increasing interest, keeping in the centre of clean ribbon of slabs (360 ft.).

Eureka, 440 ft., Very Severe. J. Grieve and E. Jones, 1967.
    A good route on superb rock taking a direct line up the front of the South Buttress. The route follows a line of grooves on the lower tier and then goes up the bulging nose above the top of the gangway. Start directly under nose of upper tier at a line of thinly defined cracks a few feet right of brown bulge at left end of lower tier. Go straight up grooves for 60 ft. until a traverse can be made to overhung slab on the left. Belay on nuts and pegs (970 ft.). Move right from stance and climb short wall to small ledge beneath steep brown groove. Climb groove to heather gangway (80 ft.). Climb directly up steep nose above and move left to pull over bulge to gain recessed slab, which climb to the right top corner. Belay (150 ft.). Climb alarmingly overhanging crack on magnificent holds (40 ft.). Finish up easy walls and ledges above (100 ft.).

South Buttress, (340 ft., Severe). The buttress at extreme right end of the West Wall; in two tiers, split by the Gangway.
    Start half-way along the steep lower wall and climb 15 ft. to a

large, obvious block belay. Move up on to slab on left, then make long traverse to right under overhangs until an ascent is possible up a smooth wall to a ledge and belay below overhangs. A broken gangway leads through the overhangs and scrambling follows to the Gangway. The upper wall is climbed to a belay below a prominent overhang which is turned by a groove on the right.

This route, the Gangway and Midgard, were done by R. B. Evans, L. A. Howarth and M. A. Evans in May 1961.

On **Taran Mor**, 996 ft., on the south side of the mouth of Loch Resort, R. Sharp and W. Sproul did a 450-ft. Severe route called *Sundowner* in 1969.

The buttresses of this hill are broken up with ledges and grass rakes and feature slabs at an easy angle. However, a deep, almost hidden gully splits the mountain and its wall gives a few pitches of steeper climbing.

Start at foot of buttress forming left gully wall at a large boulder. Climb wall into diedre and go up this to ledge with jumbled blocks. Climb up left into chimney system. Climb crack in wall and finish up slabs.

NORTH UIST

North Lee (623 ft.)
South Lee (920 ft.)
Eaval (1138 ft.)
Maps: One-inch O.S., Seventh Series, sheet 17.
　　　Half-inch Bartholomew, sheet 53.

ACCESS:
Car ferry daily from Uig, Skye (except Sunday). Car ferry on Fridays from Mallaig to Lochboisdale, South Uist. Steamer Monday, Wednesday and Friday from Oban to Lochboisdale, thence bus to Lochmaddy. Daily (except Sunday) air service from Glasgow to Benbecula.

There are hostelries at Lochmaddy (fishing; the island has one of the earliest runs of salmon in Scotland), Tigharry and Clachan).

There is a circular road – much of it a causeway – around the island, with a branch going north to Suenish on the Sound of

Berneray, and one south via the North Ford to Benbecula and Lochboisdale.

To approach either North or South Lee from Lochmaddy it is necessary to follow the road west out of the village then go a mile south along the Benbecula road before striking east across the moor, to the south of the long arm of the sea loch.

At the head of the loch is a sheep fank whose north wall, though perhaps only 20 ft. high, is absolutely perpendicular and furnished with excellent holds.

Both North and South Lee are rough and boulder-strewn but afford not unpleasant short ascents. From any of the North Uist hills in fine weather it is possible to see St. Kilda, the nearer, sandy Monachs in the western sea, and the headlands of western Skye across the Little Minch.

Eaval may be reached from the North Ford bridge in the vicinity of Carinish, going a good 6 miles eastwards by the various settlements near the south coast and up the south-west face of Eaval. One should note features along the way to ensure a return, or; from Locheport on the southern shore of Loch Eport (map reference 854635) one can continue along the road as far as Clachan Burrival and skirt the north shore of Loch Obisary, climbing over Burrival if so inclined.

Beinn Mhor (625 ft.) just east of the Newton ferry road is a good viewpoint for the Sound of Harris and the South Harris hills. C. B. Phillip wrote, 'To the southward [from Beinn Mhor] the view is truly surprising. North Uist, Benbecula and South Uist lie spread out below, literally spangled with lochs, like a long irregular strip of beautifully coloured carpet, the Lochmaddy portion in the immediate middle distance torn to fragments; the gradual change of tones from local colouring to atmosphere, as the isles recede, is on a favourable day, exquisite.'

Loch Scadavay has an area of $1\frac{3}{4}$ square miles and a shore line of 50 miles. (The circumference of a circle with area of $1\frac{3}{4}$ square miles is $4\frac{3}{4}$ miles.) Many other lochs compete in irregularity and complexity of outline. As the sign – 'Liable to subsidence' on the Lochmaddy – Benbecula road is not to be taken lightly so with map and compass work anywhere either side of it, where water in bogs and lochs predominates over the land.

There are many ancient remains hereabouts. The Chambered Cairn of Barpa Langass is one of the best, a burial construction 18 ft.

33. South Uist. Ben Mhor, Feavealloch and Hecla.

34. Mingulay. Cliffs between Ban Nish and Rudha Liath.

35. Barra. Beann Mhartuin in near distance, Heaval and Hartaval beyond.

36. Stac an Armin and Boreray.

high and 72 across, and entered by means of a tunnel. It stands near the south side of the road (A867) 6 miles west of Lochmaddy. Near the shore a short distance north-west of Carinish (map reference 816603) at Teampull na Trionaid ('of the Trinity'), are the ruins of a sixteenth-century church which was one of the most important in the Outer Isles. It is unique in having a vaulted roof. Till recently it had some fine carved stonework.

MONACH ISLES – sand swamped reefs, now uninhabited, 8 miles off the North Uist coast.

ACCESS:
Hires by fishing-boat. Enquire at Grimsay Post Office.

BENBECULA

Rueval (409 ft.)
Maps: One-inch O.S., Seventh Series, sheet 23.
Half-inch Bartholomew, sheet 53.

ACCESS:
Daily air service from Abbotsinch. Bus from Lochmaddy, North Uist, and Lochboisdale, South Uist, several times daily, except Sundays.
There is an hotel at Gramisdale, near the North Ford.

A long road bridge crosses the North Ford linking Benbecula to North Uist. Previously one had to traverse the wet sands of Oitir Mhor in the two hours during low water by a devious route of 3¾ miles close to the islet of Caigionn. The crossing is marked by stone cairns and beacons and once across the deepest part of the channel it is best to make for the summit of South Lee before turning to the north-west half a mile beyond the islet of Caigionn.

Separating South Uist and Benbecula is the South Ford, a shallow strait narrowing to half a mile where the old track crosses at low water. There is now a road bridge and the ford is seldom used. At the western end the strait is sheltered by the long, slim islet of Gualann, but at the eastern end the shallows dip steeply into 10 fathoms of water in the Bagh nam Faoileann.

Rueval, the highest hill, is close to the middle of the island. It is easily reached from the central road by a track leading into the moor, where peats are cut. W. H. Murray says: 'From the summit Benbecula looks like a well-fired crumpet pitted with holes by the hundred, the east edge nibbled away at Rossanish. The shallow seas out west are at first green then lilac in a broad band to the 10 fathom line, which lies 3½ miles offshore, thereafter indigo. To either side the spikes of the Cuillin of Skye and St. Kilda prick up from distant horizons.'

SOUTH UIST

Summits north to south are:
Ben Tarbert (549 ft.)
Hecla (1977 ft.)
Feaveallach (1723 ft.)
Beinn Mhor (2034 ft.)
Ben na Hoe (842 ft.)
Sheeval (732 ft.)
Arnaval (822 ft.)
Stulaval (1227 ft.)
Triuirebheinn (1168 ft.)
Roneval (660 ft.)

Maps: One-inch O.S., Seventh Series, sheets 23 and 32.
Half-inch Bartholomew, sheet 53.

ACCESS:
Car ferry: Mallaig–Armadale–Lochboisdale, Fridays. Steamer: Oban–Mull–Coll–Tiree–Barra–Lochboisdale. Uig, Skye – Lochmaddy and bus. Abbotsinch – Benbecula by air and bus to Lochboisdale.

ACCOMMODATION:
The principal place on the island is Lochboisdale where there is an hotel. It is 12 miles by road to the point nearest from the Beinn Mhor, the main mountain massif. At the north end there is an hotel at Carnan and an inn at Pollachar in the south.

The best approaches to the hills are either to use the driving road which runs north and south somewhat west of centre of the island, using as a base the Post Office at Loch Dobhrain (licensed) or from the Minch. Land at Corodale Bay, at the foot of Glen Hellisdale. The latter is the better route to the hills and to camp in the glen – where the Young Chevalier was well-hidden and secure from his enemies – because of the remoteness and austerity of the place, would be a much more rewarding experience.

There are three groups of hills all confined to a belt along the east side of the island. From south to north the southernmost group, between the south end of the island and Lochboisdale, consists of rounded hills, the highest of which is Easaval (*c*. 800 ft.).

Stulaval (1227 ft.), etc. The second group, standing between Loch Boisdale and Loch Eynort contains about ten hills, two of which exceed 1000 ft. in height. They are mostly grass or heather covered, with little rock showing. Stulaval, the highest is about 3 miles north of Loch Boisdale. It may be easily climbed from the hotel by following the main road out of Lochboisdale for a mile, and beyond the school at Auratote (map reference 784202) turn right and cross the north branch from Loch a Bharp by a footbridge or by the stepping-stones and follow the rough path up on to the western slope of **Triuirebheinn** to the Bealach na Diollaid, between that hill and **Clett**, and then dropping down to the east end of Loch Stulaval. Stulaval has a steep southern face but the climb to the summit is straightforward, where one has a fine view of the **Beinn Mhor** group and Loch Eynort. On the return one should traverse Triuirebheinn (1168 ft.). In the Bealach na Diollaid there is an Earth House in a good state of preservation and the remains of several stone chambers (map reference 813228), situated 300 yards N.N.E. from Loch nam Arm, quarter of a mile S.E. from Loch Stulaval. From Triuirebheinn one can continue over the Bealach an Easain (*c*. 375 ft.) to **Beinn Ruigh Choinnich** (902 ft.). The south slope is steep. The two small domed tops which may be visible due south are in Tiree, not Northern Ireland.

A return route could also be made to the north-west, down the ridge to the Hornary river and by the pools of Lochan Caorach to a track leading to the road at Mingary. To the south of the track is a chambered cairn (map reference 754260). It is 6½ miles on the road back to Lochboisdale. A quarter of a mile northwards up the road a track leads seawards to Flora Macdonald's birthplace.

Beinn Mhor (2034 ft.), **Hecla** (1988 ft.). These shapely mountains are the highest and most interesting in the Uists. They lie between Loch Eynort and Loch Skiport.

The approach to Beinn Mhor across the moor from the Post Office at Loch Dobhrain, if one heads for **Maola Breac** (939 ft.), and then follows the north-west shoulder, is surprisingly dry. It is not so short or attractive as the way in from the east coast already mentioned.

If one is making for the northern cliffs, however, which form the south wall of Coire Hellisdale one should cross the Bealach Hellisdale between Beinn Mhor and Feaveallach to the north. These cliffs are about 850 ft. high and very steep, cut into a number of bold buttresses by chimneys and gullies. The rock is gneiss. M. Botterill climbed Nos. 4 and 5 gullies in 1930 and 1932. C. Ludwig, D. Dawson and J. MacLennan climbed all buttresses and gullies in 1936. The buttresses and gullies are numbered from east to west.

No. 1 Buttress – Start at lowest rocks immediately east of Gully 2. Climb steep but fairly easy face, tending always rightwards till below overhang (about 150 ft.). Turn overhang on right and go up series of grass ledges above Gully 2. Regain crest above overhang by 15 ft. vertical pitch on small but good holds. Go up series of 20 ft. pitches with broad grass ledges between. Variants are possible east of the overhang.

No. 2 – Start west of Gully up an easy 20 ft. chimney. Pleasant face climbing for 300 ft., to 50 ft. of grass. Steep face leads to grass ledge (20 ft.). Climb crack tending right to top (80 ft.). There are two small overhangs near the top. The excellent holds make this the most enjoyable pitch of the climb.

No. 3 – The buttress is bisected by a grass terrace. The lower half offers no difficulty. Above, the buttress forms a narrow arête above Gully 4. Climb easy but fairly steep rocks (200 ft.). The angle then eases for 100 ft. Climb vertical pitch with good holds (60 ft.). Easy scrambling leads to the top (100 ft.).

No. 4 – The lower half is similar to that of No. 3 but longer and steeper. The climbing above is more difficult. The route keeps as close as possible to the edge. A vertical pitch, wet and slimy with small holds leads to grass platform (10 ft.). Climb indefinite chimney to larger grass platform (30 ft.). Steep vegetatious and rather loose rock leads to ledge below an overhang (60 ft.). Climb 10 ft. vertical wall with slimy holds to a crack tending right directly below overhang. Follow crack for about 30 ft. on vertical wall of Gully 5. Good footholds after extensive gardening. Regain ridge above overhang by press-up on to mossy ledge. Easier climbing up short steep pitches to top (200 ft.).

No. 5 – Easy grass and rock (200 ft.) to 15 ft. vertical pitch to platform below overhang. Traverse left on loose and inconveniently-placed holds till one can climb overhang up 15 ft. gutter to slimy sloping platform below final overhang. The holds improve greatly, and the remaining 30 ft. is more exposed than difficult. Owing to the absence of belays, pitons were used for protective purposes on this pitch. Several small vertical pitches with moss ledges between follow (200 ft.). The remainder of the ridge, though narrower, is at an easier angle and largely grass with short rock pitches.

No. 6 – The lower section is glaciated and holdless. Start at the mouth of Gully 7 up vertical left wall on somewhat loose holds to steeply sloping slabs on the arête (20 ft.). Climb slabs to below overhang (20 ft.). Climb overhang – steep and mossy and few holds (about 10 ft.). Climb steep and difficult and almost holdless slabs (120 ft.). (*Note*: The section from below the overhang to the end of the slabs was climbed in one run-out. Pegs were used.) Finally easy rock (100 ft.); grass (200 ft.); and grass ledges and 10 ft. vertical rock pitches (200 ft.).,

No. 7 – The narrowest and the easiest of the buttresses. The lower two-thirds of slabby rock at an easy angle. The upper third is steeper, more broken rock. Vegetatious.

The Gullies – have no special difficulty. No. 3 is steeper, rockier and drier then the rest. No. 6, though easy, is extremely slimy and should be avoided.

Between the highest top of Beinn Mhor and its north-west summit (1994 ft.) is a narrow and at one place rocky ridge half a mile long.

Northward from the Bealach Hellisdale a steep slope leads to –

Feaveallach on top of which is a large area of sound rock 100 ft. high.

This rock presents a bold scarp to the north and some care may be needed in finding the way down to the 975 bealach leading to Hecla. The rock is of good rough texture, suitable for climbing. The ascent to –

Hecla involves some 1000 ft. of climbing from the bealach, up its steep, even south face. Between the main summit and the 1820 ft. subsidiary is a 1725 ft. col. This mountain is also crowned by a bold mass of rock, but unfortunately offering little to the serious rock climber. The compass here is unreliable. Hecla is also ascended from Loch Drobhrain.

The round from Beinn Mhor to Hecla involves about 4000 ft. of ascent, but is not strenuous. It may be noticed that the rocks in the two bealachs are highly ice-worn, whilst the summit rocks are not, indicating that the Scottish ice-field which streamed out over the Outer Hebrides was not deep enough to cover the summits.

South Uist is the second largest island in the Outer Hebrides. About 21 miles from north to south with a flat and harbourless, but populated western belt and shallow sea (the ten fathom line is on an average about 3 miles from shore). There is deep water off the eastern shore, which, though it has several longer sea lochs – notably Loch Bee which goes right across the island – it is nothing like so intricate as those of the adjoining islands.

Calvay Castle ruins stand on an islet which is linked by a causeway to Calvay Island at the entrance to Lochboisdale.

1¾ miles north by the main road from Lochboisdale is a 'Chambered cairn', 86 ft. in diameter and 19 ft. high. At 8½ miles are the ruins of Ormaclett Castle, a residence of the Chief of Clanranald who ruled in South Uist till 1845.

ERISKAY

Ben Stack (403 ft.)
Ben Scrien (609 ft.)
Maps: One-inch O.S., Seventh Series, sheet 32.
Half-inch Bartholomew, sheet 53.

ACCESS:
Mail ferry between Eriskay and Ludag operated by J. Maclean, Ferry Cottage, Eriskay. Tel. Eriskay 204. From Ludag 0900 approx.

on Tuesdays, Thursdays and Saturdays. From Eriskay 1200 approx. on Mondays, Wednesdays and Fridays. Hires may be arranged with J. Maclean, or with N. Campbell, Ludag. Tel. South Boisdale 216. Hires to Eriskay from Barra (Eoligarry) may be arranged with N. Campbell.

Because there is no regular steamer service Eriskay may be reckoned the most unspoilt of all the islands with a considerable population (300), but the clearance continues: it was 420 in 1931.

Ben Stack overlooks the Sound of Barra, Ben Scrien overlooks the Sound of Eriskay. The island and its seascape are seen to great advantage from Ben Scrien – half an hour takes one to the top. Everywhere around the sandy bottom to the shallow sea gives it a luminous green colour in calm weather.

The north-west coast of Eriskay has three shell-sand bays. The south one is the Coilleag a Phrionnsa, the Prince's Beach, where Edward Stewart made his first landing on Scottish soil. Sea-convolvulus (calustega soldanella) grows near the centre on the marram fringe. It grows nowhere else in the Isles except Vatersay, near Barra.

BARRA

Heaval (1260 ft.)
Ben Tangaval (1092 ft.)
Maps: One-inch O.S., Seventh Series, sheet 32.
    Half-inch Bartholomew, sheet 53.

ACCESS:
By air from Glasgow daily. Steamer from Oban three days a week. Mallaig – Lochboisdale car ferry and steamer Lochboisdale – Castlebay, Fridays, June to September. Ludag (South Uist) to Eoligarry (Barra) by arrangement with N. Campbell, Ludag. There is a bus service operating two or three times a week – in conjunction with the steamers – between Castlebay – Green/Ersary – Eoligarry.

There is an hotel in Castlebay.

Heaval's steep but easy south-west slope may be reached if one follows the hill road which climbs the Glen before fading out at the upper end of the town (map reference 673987). From Castlebay one has little idea of the island's size, for most of it lies behind Heaval. From the top one has a better impression with rolling hills leading to the north and the wide sweep of the Borve Valley dropping to the sandy western coast. Down the south-western flank of the hill at about 850 ft. is a statue of the Virgin Mary. To the north and two-thirds of a mile west of the pass (550 ft.) between the Heiker Glen and Borve are the remains of a fine chambered cairn (map reference 677012).

A pair of standing stones will be found on the way to Borve Point. Also worth investigation in the region are the old burial ground and black houses.

Ben Tangaval's south-east ridge may be reached from Castlebay by going half a mile up the road to the head of the inlet at Bagh Beag, then turning up to the west. Half a mile up, the ridge leads to the summit.

Descending westwards takes one to the high cliffs at Doirlinn Head. Northwards from the headland a mile and a half beyond the road are the remains of Dun Ban which probably dates from the days of Viking raids. Following the coast one passes numerous exciting precipices and fierce-looking gullies. Southward, is a fine natural arch cut out by wave and wind, marked on the O.S. one-inch map.

The ascent of the five highest summits in the island from Castlebay and back makes a pleasant eleven mile round involving 3400 ft. of ascent. **Heaval** and top involves 1300 ft. of ascent; **Hartaval** and top 200 ft.; **Greanan** and **Corrabheinn** 250 ft.: then west by the 'chambered cairn' of Dun Bharpa to **Beinn Martuinn** (400 ft.): down to the coast road at sea-level and $2\frac{1}{2}$ miles along it before the final 1090 ft. to the summit of **Beinn Tangaval**, over its top and back to Castlebay.

Barra is named after Saint Barr, about whom no particulars survive.

Kiessimul Castle in Castlebay, the fortress of the Macneills, was abandoned in the eighteenth century for Eoligarry in the north of the island.

The island is about 8 miles long by $4\frac{1}{2}$ wide and is separated from South Uist by the 4-mile Sound of Barra, in which are the small islands of Hellisay, Funday, Eriskay, etc.

VATERSAY

Heishival More (625 ft.)
Ben Rulibreck (279 ft.)
Maps: One-inch O.S., Seventh Series, sheet 32.
 Half-inch Bartholomew, sheet 53.

ACCESS:
Mail ferry between Castlebay and Vatersay on Tuesdays, Thursdays and Saturdays run by H. MacLeod, 5 Vatersay. Tel. Castlebay 250. Leaves Castlebay 1030: leaves Vatersay 1100. On Mondays, Wednesdays and Fridays a mid-morning service will be run if required. Hire by arrangements.

The two hills – one in the north, the other in the south end – are connected by a narrow band of sandhills, but for which they would be separate islands. There are several other tops in the northern part.

The Sound of Vatersay between Vatersay and Barra is very narrow.

The island population, which was 250 in the thirties, is dwindling. Numbers have fallen below the marginal level that allows internal vigour and social liveliness, hence communal effort may collapse. If no new resources are found it may revert to being a single farm run from Barra, as is was before 1908.

MULDOANICH (Meall Domhnaich)

Summit 505 ft.
Maps: One-inch O.S., Seventh Series, sheet 32.
 Half-inch Bartholomew, sheet 53.

A steep-sided, hog's-backed island standing some distance out from the entrance to Castlebay. About three-quarters of a mile long it used to be kept as a deer forest. The sea eagle, now only a very rare visitor to remote cliffs in the north-east, used to nest here.

SANDRAY

Cairn Galtar (678 ft.)

Maps: One-inch O.S., Seventh Series, sheet 32.
Half-inch Bartholomew, sheet 53.

ACCESS:

No regular hirer. Enquire locally.

The island lies a mile south of Vatersay and 2½ miles north-east of Pabbay. It is 1½ miles in diameter and uninhabited. The great bank of white on the east side is a well-known seamark.

The derivation of the name is obscure. Old charts have it as Soundray.

PABBAY

The Hoe (560 ft.)

Maps: One-inch O.S., Seventh Series, sheet 32.
Half-inch Bartholomew, sheet 53.

ACCESS:

No regular hirer. Enquire locally.

The highest point is at the south-west extremity, near some high sea cliffs. Near the north end is a point over 400 ft. The east side of the island is a gradual slope with, near the shore a mass of sand rising some 300 ft. The island which is about 2 miles long by 1 wide, is roughly equidistant – 2 miles – from Sandray and Mingulay.

It is uninhabited now. In 1901 eleven people lived here. Compton Mackenzie said the bulk of the population was removed in 1840 'for distilling'.

This and the other Pabbay or Hermit's Isle in the Sound of Harris were no doubt chosen as places of religious retreat because of their isolation from the rest of the world.

MINGULAY

Macphee's Hill (736 ft.)
Carnar (891 ft.)
Maps: One-inch O.S., Seventh Series, sheet 32.
Half-inch Bartholomew, sheet 53.

ACCESS:
No regular hirer. Enquire locally.

The landing-place is in the centre of the eastern shore. The distance to Castlebay is ten miles.

The main characteristic of the island is its great cliffs which with a height of 753 ft. at Biolacraig in the south-west arc quite as impressive at the hills; particularly from seawards. A precipitous stack – Arnamul, is only a few yards from the main island on its western side. Seton Gordon found it clustered with thousands of birds and snow-white with guano.

Ornithologists say that almost everywhere the rocks are precipitous and it is in only one or two places that it is possible to climb down to where they are nesting.

Lianamul, a stack close to the west coast, is mentioned in the 1794 Statistical Account which says that the Mingulay people climb to the top of it 'at the risk of their lives, and by means of a rope carry up their wedders to fatten'. The stack was once connected to Mingulay by a rope bridge according to Harvie-Brown. This had disappeared before his first visit in 1871. The landing place was at the southern end on the seaward side. He said the climb was a severe one, though he had neither done it himself nor seen it done.

There are several 'sea arcades' winding their way amongst the cliffs and promontories. The Gunamul natural arch, whose adjoining cliff is 504 ft. high is marked on the six-inch map.

Mingulay (Bird Island) is the penultimate isle of the Barra group and the third largest. It is $2\frac{3}{4}$ miles long by $1\frac{1}{2}$ wide. It held a population of around 140 at the turn of the century. In 1908 the people were moved to Vatersay, leaving a township still to be seen, derelict on the east coast.

Macphee of the Hill was put ashore on the island to get news of the inhabitants and report back to MacNeil of Barra. He found everyone dead of the plague. The other members of the crew would not allow him back aboard and he spent a year on the island climbing the Hill every day looking for rescue.

Perhaps 'a Macphee' might become the name for the person who only wants to do one mountain as opposed to a 'Munroist' who wants to do all the mountains.

BERNERAY (Bjorn's Isle)

Summit, 631 ft.
Maps: One-inch O.S., Seventh Series, sheet 32.
Half-inch Bartholomew, sheet 53.

ACCESS:
No regular hirer. Enquire locally. A passage may possibly be obtained on the lighthouse tender from Castlebay.

The island lies half a mile south of Mingulay. It is $1\frac{3}{4}$ miles long and three-quarters of a mile wide, and rears up to its final buttress at Barra Head, the most southerly point of the Outer Hebrides. There are magnificent cliffs on the western side which take the brunt of gigantic seas, for there is no shallow water here to trip and impede the great Atlantic rollers.

Near the lighthouse – 683 ft. above high-water – there is a chasm in the cliffs 100 yards long by 600 ft. deep leading to a cave yet to be explored. Two duns are situated near the summit of the isle, the site of a chapel is near the landing-place, and there is a 'chalybeate spring' about half-way up by the side of the track. The cove east of the landing-place is much frequented by grey seal.

REFERENCES

Carmina Gadelica. Report for the Crofter's Commission, 1883.
The Scenery of Scotland, Sir Archd. Geikie.
Itinerary of Prince Charles Edward Stuart. (Scottish History Society, vol 23.)
The Truth about Flora Macdonald. (The Northern Chronicle, Inverness).

A vertebrate Fauna of the Outer Hebrides, Brown, Buckley and Heddle.
The Children of the Tempest, Neil Munro.
Scottish Place Names, K. P. MacKenzie.
North Uist, Erskine Beveridge (1911).
The Norseman in Alban, R. L. Bremner, 1923. Maclehose.
The Islands of Scotland, Hugh MacDairmid.
The Outer Isles, A. Goodrich-Freer.
The Book of The Lews, W. C. MacKenzie.
Harpoon at a Venture, Gavin Maxwell.
Songs of the Hebrides, Mrs. Kennedy Fraser.
Father Allan's Island, Miss Amy Murray.
Whisky Galore, Compton Mackenzie.
Isles of Lewis and Harris, A. Geddes, 1955.
Castle in the Sea, MacNeil of Barra.
The Book of Barra, J. L. Campbell.
The Hebrides, W. H. Murray.
The *Scottish Mountaineering Club Journal* –
  Vol. 6, p. 147, 'North Uist' by Colin B. Philip.
     12, p. 256, Harris. Clisham, etc., by E. G. Farquhar.
     20, p. 79, The Mountains of South Uist by J. A. Parker.
     22, p. 184, The Furthest Hebrides, by E. W. Hodge.
     24, p. 52, A Note on the Climbing in Harris by E. Rudge.
     24, p. 308, Hill Crossing to Harris by J. McCallum Young.
     28, p. 227, A 3400 ft. Round in Barra, by R. G. Inglis.
     29, p. 26, Strone Ulladale, by J. Grieve.

NEW CLIMBS:
  Vol. 27, p. 265,
       28, pp. 211, 277.
       29, p. 280, 48
Yorkshire Rambler's Club Journal, Vol. 6, p. 17. Sgurr Scaladale by
M. Botterill.

7
The Outermost Isles

Haskier, Monach Isles, St. Kilda, The Flannan Isles, North Rona, Sula Sgeir, Sule Stack and Rockall.

HASKIER

Haskier Mhor Summit (142 ft.)
Haskier Eagach (notched Haskier)
Maps: One-inch O.S., Seventh Series, sheet 17.
Half-inch Bartholomew, sheet 53.
Admiralty Chart 2474.

These are two groups of precipitous rocks, near each other and about 8 miles south-west of Griminish Point, North Uist.

Landing is difficult. No regular service. Hires by fishing boat may be arranged, enquire at Grimsay Post Office. Tel. Grimsay 402.

Haskier Eagach, which lies perhaps a mile to the south-west of the Mhor, consists of five distinct islets or stacks, which rise close together with deep-water channels between.

On the north-west shore of Haskier Mhor is a splendid rocky bay. The lowest land lies at the centre of the island. In the north is a high sea-cliff knows as the Castle; in the south is a rounded hill. Between is a natural arch, over which one can walk without difficulty. The sea pinks, campion and sea plantain are of an unusual size. There is no grass. The islands are a grey seal sanctuary.

THE MONACH ISLES lie 12 miles to the south of Haskier, to which the remarks on maps and access apply.

They are machair dunes less than 50 ft. high protected by reefs, 6 miles west of North Uist. Ceann Ear (East Head) – inhabited till 1942 – is joined at low tide to Ceann Iar (West Head) and another islet. The lighthouse is on the Shillay rock on the west side, which has a spit running south from it known as 'The Panhandle'. A small cliff on the western side has a deep cleft in the centre.

ST. KILDA GROUP

Conachair (1397 ft.)
Mullach Mor (1172 ft.)
Dun Island (576 ft.)
Stac Levenish (185 ft.)
Soay (1114 ft.)
Stac na Biorrach (236 ft.)
Bororay (1245 ft.)

Maps: One-inch O.S., sheet 17. The six-inch O.S., revised in 1963, is the best map available of the whole group.
Admiralty Charts, 2474, 2721, 2335, 1144 (Plan of Village Bay).

The St. Kilda Group lies about 52 miles due west from North Uist; lat. 57° 50'N.; 8° 30'W. It consists of three main islands – Hirta, Soay and Bororay.

ACCESS:
Permission from the National Trust, the Nature Conservancy and the Army is needed to visit St. Kilda. It is probably best to make individual arrangements to go with official trips, otherwise nothing but well sponsored and backed operations will have much encouragement. The chances of not being able to land, even in summer, are fairly high.

At low water boats cannot normally go alongside the old pier on the northern side of Village Bay, which is the main anchorage for St. Kilda, owing to thick seaweed and heavy boulders on the bottom. Alterations are being made which will be published in Notices to Mariners.

On the north side of Hirta (the main island) is a small indentation – Glen or Gleann Bay. It is well sheltered from the north, but is not comfortable owing to the swell. It is used when a south-easterly gale is blowing into Village Bay. From the head of Glen Bay a straight valley runs south-eastward between the hills, and the stream through it runs into the head of the bay at a place where the cliffs are sufficiently sloping to permit landing. Landing is occasionally possible near one of the caves on the northern coast. It is almost never possible to land on the southern coast on account of the surf.

Village Bay is protected from winds up to about strength 4, except from north-east and south-east. Swell is caused by strong south-westerly winds. During gales, squalls from the hills are unpredictable and very violent though only momentary. Gusts of over 130 m.p.h. have been recorded. The holding ground is good. Sand.

From the vicinity of North Uist, the group has the appearance of a number of pillars on the horizon, but as a vessel approaches it becomes a distinct group of mountains rising straight up out of the sea. Mist or fog often prevent the islands being seen until within a distance of 5 miles or less.

The group consists chiefly of two igneous rocks, a light coloured granite or granophyre and a darker gabbro. The eastern part of Hirta is chiefly granite; the dark parts and the ragged pinnacles on the other islands – mainly Boraray – are gabbro. Some of the rock is highly magnetic. The coastline of all the islands is honeycombed with caves.

The 1549 Munro said of the place – 'at the Schoir side of it lyis three great hills, quhilk are ane pairt of Hirt, quhilk are seen far off from the forlands. In thir rock Iles are infinite fair scheippis with ane falcon nest and wild foullis biggard. But the seais are stark and verie evill.'

MacAulay thought the people had been tarred and feathered; the birds and fulmar oil were all pervading.

A lot has been written about the native tradition of climbing. It was not done for fun but for the frankly utilitarian purposes of catching sea-birds or a wife. It may seem a strange idea – that good climbers make good husbands. 'Quel metier!' as cartoonist Samivel said. The test was the ability to balance on one leg at the edge of a precipice on Ruaival; dither on the brink with disaster either way. The alternative of remaining single might well be preferred.

A process of natural selection seems to have controlled the few fatalities in climbing. Those who died in this way being thought neither strong enough mentally nor physically to be of lasting use to the community.

The birds along with some wool were the main resources of the islands. The feathers were gathered to be sold by their agent in Glasgow up till the evacuation in 1930; the oil likewise, which was extracted from the sack in the fulmar's neck. The carcases of all birds were eaten, including the fulmars, but the young gannets and puffins were the favourites. When Martin Martin visited the island in 1697 he estimated that the St. Kildans ate 16,000 eggs per week and some 22,600 birds were eaten annually. Lee Stac alone provided between five and seven thousand gannets a year. Rye grass and barley, which were the main crops, had to be cut green. They were stored and dried in the wonderful bee-hive shaped stone buildings – the cleats or 'cleitean'.

Nothing was known of the St. Kildans prior to Martin Martin's visit and it is an interesting question how the people came there in the first place. A pre-viking settlement has been found in Gleann Bay by Dr. Iain Whittaker of the school of Scottish Studies.

There is no single island that bears the name St. Kilda and the origin of the name is a subject of controversy. Martin Martin called it quite categorically St. Kilda. In the Celtic 'hiort' (Hirta) meant death or gloom.

At present Hirta is occupied by army personnel, contractors men, and a warden, the latter not in permanent residence. A representative of the National Trust calls from time to time, and National Trust parties periodically visit the island to maintain the antiquities.

After a visit to assess the possibilities of a direct ascent of the 1300 ft. cliff face of Conachair, on Hirta, Tom Patey wrote rather discouragingly – 'We were marooned for three weeks of continuous gales, snow and rain, during which we did nothing but look for a sail.

'Climbing on St. Kilda is not an easy business. You may be marooned for a month. Even having got there you won't find anything to do without a boat; then only on the average three days a month when you can land on the stacks or Bororay.

'During the nesting months, these are plastered knee-deep in excrement, hence the quality of the underlying rock is purely an academic point. In winter, when the rocks are clean, it's too rough to land at the bottom. Again, anything really good – and there's much less then you might think – is so steep I would doubt if you could make any major free climbs in the place. "Pitoneers" would find a lot to do. The rock is good granite where you get down to it. Remember to take crampons and ice-axe if you go. Getting to any of the routes would probably involve traversing short cropped grass at an enormous angle and the result is rather like snow climbing.

'No wonder the original St. Kildans had prehensile, divergent toes!'

HIRTA

Conachair 1397 ft.

Hirta is all steeply angled turf in the bowl surrounding Village Bay. It is an island of two glens flanked by high steep hills. Though there are no trees or shrubs on the island the hills are green from the bottom of the glens to their summits. Village Glen is dominated in the east by **Oiseval** (948 ft.), and the symetrical cone of **Conachair** in the middle. Other tops are **Mullach Mor** (1172 ft.), **Mullach Bi** (1164 ft.), and **Mullach Sgar** (715 ft.). **Ruaival** lies opposite Dun islet, forming the southern end of the horseshoe. Between **Mullach Geal** and **Mullach Sgar** is a col – Am. Blaid 740 ft. from which one can look down the wide 'U' of Gleann Mor, enclosed on the inland side by Mullach Mor, and on the west by the serrated coastal ridge of Mullach Bi. In Gleann Mor, rather more than half-way down, is a cleit which will take two in sleeping bags. Dr. J. Eggeling, an ornithologist, when he spent the night here had two Leach's petrels courting on his chest.

Conachair is reached from Village Bay by a steep slope of well-cropped grass. There is now a road running to within a mile of the cliff edge. There is a bog at the top, but the footing is secure at the cliff edge. Tom Weir and Douglas Scott descended the face of the sea cliff to the overhang above the sea. They found the rocks generally safe. It was the grass slopes that were awkward, and these usually end in small but steep and dangerously loose cliffs, about which the sheep scamper with wonderful assurance. A short ice-axe is useful for climbers with only two legs. Scott and Weir used camera tripods.

There should be several good lines up the seaward side of Conachair apart from the one directly up the centre.

On the cliffs of Conachair the birds were supposedly so densely packed that the St. Kildan fowler normally had to kill them in order

to make his way along the ledges. One wonders how Weir and Scott –
who are meant to be bird-lovers – managed.

From Ruaival, the extreme southernmost point there is a fine
view of the western cliffs and a good approach to the west coast is
over the lowest point in the saddle between Mullach Sgar and Ruaival. The rocks about six cables north-west of Ruaival summit offer
an easy line of descent, but some care is needed in the central section
which consists of a band of lighter coloured looser rock. There is
good scrambling in the region of Ruaival on sound gabbro, and some
splendid traverses or 'crab-crawls' could be done above the swell
line.

Dun or Duin Island (576 ft.).

Landing can be affected on the Village Bay side in calm weather close
to the cave at the north-western end, on to a steeply shelving granite
ledge. Without a boat, reaching the stac would involve swimming
even at low water though the passage is only a few yards. On the stac
itself there is still a chain of doubtful security. R. Hillcoat reported
landing on Dun in adverse conditions a nightmare.

Culminating at its south-eastern end in Boida More, the ridge is
named Goban an Duin on which, according to 'The Admiralty'
Pilot, there are the crumbling ruins of a castle. There is, however,
no trace of it now. It was probably so named for its shape. The outline of this island is serrated in a fantastic manner, the south-western
slope is precipitous and indented, the north-eastern a steep green
slope. Goban an Duin is penetrated by a natural tunnel through
which the sea flows. The passage is not safe for boats.

Following the crest of the ridge, which from Village Bay is like the
Cuillin of Skye in miniature, involves the ascent of some airy pinnacles if not hard climbing. There is a lot of scope for scrambling
on the rocky southern side, but erosion makes access difficult and
trap dykes are much in evidence here. Long tufty grass on the Village
Bay side makes heavy going – there are no sheep on Dun.

St. Kilda wren, and puffin in large numbers, nest here. Stac
Levenish, 185 ft. high, is one mile east of Dun. Its shape is pyramidal.
The stac is only of navigational significance.

Soay, (1114 ft.), is separated by a strait 400 yards from the west-north-western end of Hirta. It is a flattish grassy incline on top, terminating on the south in high vertical cliffs and is cliff-girt all round. The landing-place is at the south-eastern end.

The channel between Soay and Biorrach is deep but has several rocks in it.

Stac na Biorrach (pron. 'peerich') 236 ft. – and nearby Stac Dona lie in the channel between Soay and St. Kilda, close east of the eastward side of Soay. There is a deep channel at the north-western end of St. Kilda navigable in fine weather.

This stac offers some of the best possibilities for climbing in the group.

The first to climb this stac and Stac Lee – apart from the native St. Kildans – was Charles Barrington in 1883, who also made the first ascent of the Eiger. See the *Alpine Journal*; Vol. xxvii, p. 195, also Heathcote's *St. Kilda*.

Barrington describes the landing as difficult, and it was followed by a severe pitch of 40 ft. on the western face leading to a stance 18 inches square (belay). Next an easterly rake led to a hand-traverse with a 'thumb-hold'. When a pinnacle about 80 ft. from sea-level had been lassoed, the main difficulty was past.

Sir Robert Moray's account of this climb written in 1698 is surely the first description we have of any rock-climb in Scotland.

At that time: 'after they landed, a man having room for but one of his feet, he must climb up 12 or 16 fathoms high. Then he comes to a place where having but room for his left foot and left hand, he must leap from thence to another place before him, which if hit right the rest of the ascent is easy, and with a small cord which he carries with him he hales up a rope whereby all the rest come up. But if he misseth that footstep (as often times they do) he falls into the sea and the (boat's) company takes him in and he sits still until he is a little refreshed and then he tries it again, for everyone there is not able for that sport'.

Bororay 1245 ft. with its close neighbours Stac Lee and Stac an Armin, form a separate group 4 miles north-east of St. Kilda.

There is a deep channel free from dangers between Stac Lee and the western side of Bororay. The channel between Bororay and Stac an Armin is full of rocks and cannot be used even by small boats.

Approaching Village Bay from the east, the east and south-west ridges of Bororay are reminiscent of the Fünfingerspitze (Cinque Dita) of the Dolomites with only three fingers.

Williamson and Boyd where they landed, left a peg, and a short distance above came to a *mauvais pas* – a chasm which breaks the continuity of the southern crags. It is 5 ft. at the narrowest point – to be jumped. The sea surges 100 ft. below, but there is a secure belay.

On Bororay there is little hard substrata that is not actually vertical. From the west summit there is seen the sheer might and astounding grandeur of cliff, sea and sky and seafowl. The east ridge is also very fine.

Landing on Bororay, according to R. Balharry who visited it with Morton Boyd, was easy enough after the struggles they had had on Stac Lee and Stac an Armin, with no more than scree and slippery grass for a thousand feet to the top.

He recommends the Cathedral Spire as a climb.

There are still traces of lazy beds on top of Bororay, where potatoes were grown. By 1889 the St. Kildans were visiting the island only three times a year.

Stac Lee 544 ft. lies about 600 yards west of Bororay.

It looks formidable when approaching Village Bay, like a huge black iceberg on the point of toppling.

From the south end of Bororay the more gently angled side can be seen, and is a moderate route to the top of a series of shelves.

It is, along with Stac an Armin, the only nesting place of the gannets on St. Kilda.

On the relatively level top there is a solid concentration of over 6,000 nests. The gannets had always to be taken at night, and the sentry bird – who remained awake and would give the alarm as soon as his suspicions were aroused – had to be killed first. His slaughter in fact was the most awkward part of the work.

Balharry and Boyd who climbed Stac Lee in 1969, landed at a point near the south-eastern corner of the stac. Balharry says:

'According to the books, the St. Kildans lassoed an iron peg, then a man was hauled up from the boat. The tradition is of a difficult landing, and we had on our life-jackets. When the moment came that the boat was on the highest swell we stepped out, found slippery hand and footholds and began climbing. We didn't waste time. It was near vertical, but there were plenty of holds, and in twenty feet we were on a ledge.

'The first hundred feet was easy enough, but the bit beyond was a different story. You looked straight down to the sea, and the only way above was up a blank wall.

'It looked impossible. The weathered rock seemed to have been swept away by a rockfall, leaving only smoothness behind. I was on a six-inch ledge, and banged in a piton for security. If I could traverse fifteen feet of that wall to the far edge I felt I might get somewhere.

'I inched out on no more than balance holds, feeling I could retire if necessary. But not on the last six feet. The last move could not be tested because it needed a long reach and a long stride, then it needed a sideways pull across to the shattered edge.

'The birds were screaming like an excited crowd at a football match. Straight below was the sea, the orange life-jackets, and the boats like tiny slugs. The next bit was actually overhanging, then in another twenty feet I was on a ledge with a good belay.

'We were now on a great bevelled roof of gannets and walking up the ledges of slimy guano you sank in at every step. Now and again gannets would reach out and grip your arm in their beaks.

'There was a small bothy on top, beautifully dry inside, and capable of holding two men, but two fulmars had taken over.'

Of the descent he says:

'I was right in my assumption that I would not be able to reverse the hard move, and I was forced to hammer a peg into the brittle rock and rope-down. The second peg went "home" after the first had loosened six feet of rock which thundered down.'

Stac an Armin, 627 ft., lies 300 yards off Bororay's north-western point. It is the highest sea stac in the British Isles, climbed by R. Balharry, C. Welsh and M. Boyd in May 1969. Their only difficulty was in landing; the ascent was easy.

This is probably the first time the stac has been climbed since the departure of the St. Kildans who used to visit it annually to harvest the gannets.

It was on this stac that the last great auk in Britain was killed, beaten to death in July 1840 by two St. Kildans who thought it was a witch.

THE FLANNAN ISLES

Eilan Mor 283 ft. high.
Gaealtare Mor

Maps: One-inch O.S., Seventh Series, sheet 12.
Half-inch Bartholomew, sheet 57.
Admiralty chart 2386, plan 3331.

The most likely way of reaching the islands is by fishing boat from Lewis, or by the lighthouse vessel. The fishermen visit the islands to take 'gougas' (2-year-old gannets). Landing can only be attempted in moderate weather and the best place is the south-western shore of Eilan Mor.

Consisting of several islands forming three distinct groups, they lie 20 miles west by north from Gallan Head, Lewis, Lat. 58° 17′ N., Long. 7° 36′ west. Eilan Mor the largest carries the lighthouse whose height is 330 ft. above high water. The isles are uninhabited except for lighthousemen. Gaealtare More is the easternmost. The tops are grassy but cliffbound on all sides. On top of Eilan Mor is the 'Chapel of St. Flannan' and some primitive dwellings.

They are also known as the Seven Hunters and the North Hunters. The rock is gneiss.

Martin Martin gives an interesting account of the procedures observed and the superstitions held by the Lewis people who went wildfowling in the Flannan Islands. We will forbear from quoting.

NORTH RONA

Summit 355 ft.

Maps: One-inch O.S., Seventh Series, sheet 8.
Half-inch Bartholomew, sheet 58.
Admiralty chart 2635 and 1954.

44 miles N.N.E. from the Butt of Lewis, and 45 miles N.W. from Cape Wrath, Lat. 59° 7′ N., Long. 5° 50′ W.

Landing is difficult. The best place is on the northern side of the hill, or in a small creek in its southern side according to the direction of the wind. A landing has been effected on the eastern side of the northern point of the island.

Measuring about one mile either way, North Rona is generally undulating turfy moor, but at the south-eastern end rises steeply to point 355 ft. with a vertical cliff to the south. At the north end the sea has piled a vast number of boulders forming an embankment 70 or 80 ft. high along the north-western coast. Water flung over this has in streaming down eastwards to the sea, cut deep channels through the turf to the bed-rock.

One might join the party which visits the island annually – usually at the end of July – to gather the sheep. North Rona has been uninhabited since 1844.

SULA SGEIR or SULISKER

222 ft. high (Pilot).

Maps: One-inch O.S. Seventh Series sheet 8.
    Half-inch Bartholomew, sheet 58.

Lies 12 miles west-south-west from North Rona. Lat. 59° 6′ N., Long. 6° 10′ W. It measures half a mile by under 200 yards. A precipitous islet, it has scarcely any surface soil but plants grow in the crevices, some abundantly.

The south-eastern and north-western sides should not be approached too closely.

There is a colony of thousands of gannets on the island and every summer men from Ness in Lewis spend a fortnight there catching and salting down the 'gougas'.

GRALISGEIR is a rock showing just above water off the southern extremity of Sula Sgeir.

SULA STACK or STACK SKERRY, 130 ft. 32 miles north of Loch Eriboll, Darness.

37. St. Kilda. Conachair, Hirta. Bird-watcher's nests in foreground.

38. St. Kilda. Stac Dun.

39. St. Kilda. Soay Stac and Stac Biorrach with Soay in the
background.

40. Orkney. The Old Man of Hoy. The cairns were built after the first ascent.

SULE SKERRY, 40 ft. high.

Five miles north-east of Sule Stack Lighthouse. It forms part of the ballad: 'I am the selchie (seal) of Sule Skerry.'

The Skerries are shown on Admiralty charts 1954 and 2635.

ROCKALL, 70 ft. approx.

Admiralty chart for North Atlantic.

In Lat. 57° 33′ N., Long. 13° 40′ W., 226 miles west of North Uist. Rockall is farther from land than any other known rock of such small size – it is about 83 ft. across at sea-level. A lone tusk – the last sign for 3,000 sea miles of a vanishing continent.

Landing even in the finest weather is difficult, and the rock has only been ascended on its north-east side.

Twenty miles beyond St. Kilda is the hundred fathom line from which the sea-bed drops to 1000 fathoms and more. It then rises to the Rockall bank, famed for halibut. Rockall is the summit of a submarine mountain, shaped like a haystack with steep walls, sloping roof and level summit ridge.

The first recorded ascent was made in 1810 by members of Captain Basil Hall's ship's company, who brought away a piece of rock – a coarse granite. In 1862 the rock was visited by H.M.S. *Porcupine* and the boatswain landed, but at a place from which the summit could not be reached. The captain of a Grimsby trawler landed and climbed to the top in 1888. Transactions of the Royal Irish Academy for 1896–1901 give an account of an expedition to Rockall. They failed to land, but took soundings, dredgings, photographs, and made sketches. The bird population then was 250 guillemots, 50 kittiwakes, 30 puffins and 10 gannets.

The present writer has never climbed this rock, but he can claim to have seen it despite his experience, when, as a novice-navigator he was ordered to hit Rockall – no mean task with the sea so rough that the cat was as sick as a dog. He was flung from his bunk and with his nose, hit the gyro compass instead. The captain angrily told him he'd broken his only piece of reliable navigational apparatus, and that was the second time his nose had been broken.

REFERENCES

Carminica Gadelica.
Macculloch. Vol. iii.
A Hundred Years of Life in the Highlands. Osgood Mackenzie, contains a chapter on a voyage to St. Kilda.
A Vertebrate Fauna of the Outer Hebrides, Harvey-Brown and Buckley.
St. Kilda, G. Seton. Blackwood (1877).
The Life and Death of St. Kilda, Tom Steele. (National Trust for Scotland.)
The Songs of Craig and Ben, Dr. A. Geddes.
A Mosaic of Islands, K. Williamson and M. Boyd.
St. Kilda Summer, K. Williamson and M. Boyd.
Atlantic Fury, Hammond Innes.
Pincher Martin (Rockall), William Golding.
Ronay, M. Stewart (1933, Rona Sula Sgeir, Flannan, Monach, Shiant).
A Naturalist on Rona, Dr. F. Fraser Darling (1939).
St. Kilda, N. Heathcote
Report of Ancient Monuments Commission – Outer Isles.
Island Going, R. Atkinson (1949).
Scots Magazine. September, 1969. Article by R. Balharrie and T. Weir on St. Kilda.
Geographical Magazine. 'Birds and Men on St. Kilda' by Dr. Julian Huxley.
The *Scottish Mountaineering Club Journal:*
    Vol. 6, p. 146, 'Climbing in St. Kilda' by N. Heathcote.
    21, pp. 255, 429.
    22, pp. 184, 130.
The *Alpine Journal* – Vol. 27, p. 195, 'The ascent of Stack-na-Biorrach' by R. M. Barrington.

8

The Orkneys and Shetlands

The North of Scotland and Orkney and Shetland Steam Navigation Company serves both groups, and has its head office at Matthew's Quay, Aberdeen. There are twice-weekly services from Leith and Aberdeen to Kirkwall (Orkney) and Lerwick (Shetland): also twice weekly sailings from Aberdeen direct to Shetland.

From Scrabster to Stromness there is a daily service (including Sundays in July and August).

There are flights daily from Glasgow, Edinburgh, Aberdeen and Inverness to Kirkwall and Lerwick. Logan-Air run charter flights between Wick and Orkney, and service flights within the islands.

In both groups of islands, the profiles are flat on top or rounded even where they rise high. The Orkneys consist almost entirely of the Old Red Sandstone, whose strata are inclined usually at a gentle angle, and with only a few basaltic dykes, but the Shetlands have great variety of rock. Both groups have some magnificent sea-cliffs. In Orkney and Shetland cliff-climbing was not much indulged in even when H. Raeburn wrote about the islands in 1910 in the *Scottish Mountaineering Club Journal*.

Since the type of rock is the best guide to climbing areas, geological map numbers have been given. On the whole the granite is to be sought-out, the sandstone avoided.

The Orkneys and Shetlands not only have a western climate due to the influence of the Gulf Stream, but have the sunshine record for the British Isles. Though Orkney is nearer to the Arctic Circle than it is to London, extending to within 25 miles of the Latitude of Cape Farewell in Greenland, the winter temperature is the same as that of the Isle of Wight and higher than that of London. The average rainfall is from 30 to 35 inches per year.

Though bare and treeless, the moors can be covered with the blur of wild lupins and the rare primula Scotica is to be found.

Since almost all the place-names and words referring to natural objects are of Norse origin some notes on these are useful to climbers.

Bay, *hope*, *wick* or *voe* – sea inlet.

Loch – inland water.

Sounds or *firths* – large sea-channels.

Geos – small breaks in the coast eroded by sea action, often continued inland as sea-tunnels.

Gloups – sea-tunnels terminating in open holes whereby the air compressed by the water escapes, or where the water itself is thrown upwards.

Brough – a part of cliff that having withstood wave action stands out as a bold peninsula, sometimes approachable at low tide only.

Castle – a completely isolated stack, not necessarily with anything built upon it.

Hamar – steeper part of a hillside where the terraces of rock emerge, alternating with scree.

Ward – watch, e.g. Ward Hill, means watch hill, sometimes with fire beacon.

THE ORKNEY ISLANDS

Mainland, Hoy, Rousay and Westray are dealt with here as being the most interesting to climbers.

Maps: One-inch O.S., Seventh Series, sheets 5, 6 and 11.
      Half-inch Bartholomew, sheet 61.
      Quarter-inch Geological Survey, sheet 3.

The *Earl of Thorfinn* which sails to the North Isles from Kirkwall is to be replaced by a hydrofoil service. With a speed of 32 knots these boats should considerably reduce the time taken to go from one island to another. There is a steamer service from Stromness to the southern islands of the group. The s.s. *Hoy Head* runs with mails to Graemsay, Hoy, Cava, Faray, Flotta and Longhope.

In either archipelago the wealthy climber will probably find it much to his advantage to hire a boat for visiting islands, thereby having a much more flexible timetable.

Of the 68 Orkney islands, some 29 are inhabited.

Mainland

(Mistakenly called Pomona by G. Buchanan, a seventeenth-century latinist: Meginland to the early Norse settlers.)

Ward Hill of Orphir (881 ft.)
Wideford Hill (741 ft.)

The largest island of the group, Mainland has the two most important towns, Kirkwall and Stromness, 15 miles west. Kirkwall has Tankerness House, Earl's Palace, St. Magnus Cathedral and Bishop's Palace. Stromness has an interesting museum and is the port for Scrabster. Both towns have hotels.

The island is about 30 miles long, but only $1\frac{1}{2}$ miles wide between Kirkwall Bay and Scapa Flow.

A fine panorama is to be had from *Wideford Hill* at the back of Kirkwall, rewarding the climber out of all proportion to its height. Hoxa Sound is visible at the southern end leading to the 'worst patch of water in the world' – the Pentland Firth.

Beyond may be seen Dunnet Head and the Morven peaks on a clear day. It also commands a fine view of Kirkwall Bay and the northern islands.

Just above Stromness, at Brinkies Brae is the oldest place geologically in Orkney. The Dalriadan granite rock was once an island in a great freshwater loch.

The ascent of Wideford Hill might well be combined with a visit to a large underground dwelling with beehive roof a mile to the north-east.

From Stromness the walk (about 15 miles) along the Atlantic coast can be recommended. 'En route' are the Black Craig – a line of savage cliffs, the rock stacks of N. Gaulton and Yesnaby Castles and 8 miles farther on, a natural arch. Near Scaill Bay a mile further is the famous Pictish village of Skara Brae, excavated between 1927 and 1932 by Professor Gordon Childe. At Birsay (hotel) is the ruined palace of the jarls. The Brough of Birsay, a half-tide island, has traces of a broch and an ancient church.

North Gaulton Castle, 150 ft., was climbed in 1970 by P. Minks and C. Phillips. The ascent took three hours. Two companions then linked up with them by means of a traverse rope from the nearest headland, 150 ft. away.

The Gloup of Deerness which lies on the east coast near Deer

Sound just east of Kirkwall, is a great gash in the rocks, 70 yards long by 40 yards wide connected to the sea by an underground fissure.

On South Ronaldsay, south of Mainland, 9 miles from Scapa Flow, where indigenous sheep now live, the Maid of Norway died long ago. West is Flotta across the Sound of Hoxa. The island of Burray, just to the north, has a fine Pictish broch.

HOY

Knap of Trewiglen (1308 ft.)
Ward Hill (1565 ft.)
Cuilags (1420 ft.)

There are daily boat sailings to Lyness from Stromness, and on Mondays and Fridays, from Scapa. Boats may be hired from A. G. Brown & Son, Tel. Stromness 240, to various points of Hoy such as the Old Man. The shortest crossing is to Linksness where there is a pier, which is the best centre for the hills and the western cliffs.

Hoy is next in size to the Mainland and is the highest and much the wildest of the Orkney isles. It is about 13 miles long excluding the almost-detached peninsula of Walls. There are some 250 inhabitants. On its north-west coast is a 12-mile stretch of beetling cliffs. St. John's Head, 1141 ft. is one of the highest sea-cliffs in the British Isles. Nearby is the famous Old Man of Hoy (450 ft.). The Ward Hill of Hoy is the highest in Orkney. The high ground of the isle rises in three masses, divided by gaps at least 1000 ft. deep, with Ward Hill in the middle.

The summit of the **Knap of Trewiglen** is readily reached from the top of the road from the Bay of Quoys to the Dwarfie Stone, up the Trowie Glen. The Dwarfie Hamars may be investigated on the way.

Ward Hill is most easily ascended from its N.W. side. There is a spring near the westernmost of the two cairns on its flattish top. From its top the whole archipelago may be seen, even to North Ronaldsay 50 miles north and Fair Isle beyond. On the steep north side of Ward Hill there was supposed to be a great carbuncle which gleamed a ruddy red in the dark, but which disappeared before you could reach it. To the south-east is a deep corrie, the Nowt Bield (a sheltered place for cattle).

After climbing to the summit of the **Cuilags** there is very little height lost before St. John's Head is reached. The winds here are strong enough to have torn great slabs from their beds at the cliff edge and hurled them several yards inland.

In July 1970 Edwin Ward Drummond and Oliver Hill spent two days descending the face and five ascending to the top of St. John's Head. They wish it to be known as the Longhope Route, in memory of the life-boat disaster, though at the other end of the island.

St. John's Head is split from the mainland by a 50-ft. notch which gives an easy scramble.

Anthony Greenbank, who went to 'cover' the climb for the *Sunday Telegraph* and assist said:

'The only way to reach the beach below St. John's Head is to abseil from top to bottom. As the two ropes swung 30 ft. clear of the face on the first 700 ft. of overhangs, the wind kept dragging them horizontally over the sea, making descent impossible. So I was lowered on the ends as ballast to a grass ledge 600 ft. below. Only snag – the wind kept spinning me round crossing the two ropes like the rubber band in a model aeroplane. Untwisting them from below proved impossible, and Drummond had an epic fight to get down, for the rope twisted above him as well as below. Half-way down he started to spin crazily, helicopter-blade fashion, in thin air. We could do nothing and he started to turn upside-down. Then, with tremendous determination, he began to pull kink after kink in the two ropes apart and climbed through each gap created. Two hours later he was down shaken and exhausted.

'Another fright had happend when Hill was lowered – tied also to two 80 lb. haul-bags. The karabiner through which Drummond was paying out the rope grew so hot that the line, in this case Ulstron as used by yachtsmen, started to melt and come apart under the terrific load. Frantically Drummond reached for some dock leaves and squeezed their juice over the scorching metal. It cooled the situation – just.'

Edwin Ward Drummond continues the narrative:

FRIDAY. On the first pitch; 'at the end of 120 ft. I am almost in tears The sandstone is so damned dangerous. I creep off on the second pitch, which isn't too bad and brings me to a big ledge with a rock roof over our heads.

SATURDAY. 'Six hours after [breakfast] I stitch my way through a maze of traverses across the face to exit at a superb grass ledge to be greeted by a clutch of butterflying puffins, nodding as coolly as dons in the afternoon sun as I fist-jam my way past them.

'We sleep on another lush ledge, slightly higher, which we name the House of Lords.

SUNDAY. 'We awake to the black shadow of the North Wall printed on the sea 500 ft. below us. Presently I climb Vile Crack, 100-ft. long and the nastiest size for a climber to cope with, because too wide to be ascended by jamming hands or feet in, I climb it with precarious pressure-holds and foot scrapes, and find I have to top it with a traverse on a ledge of window-sill thickness.

MONDAY. 'Oliver has crossed the Forever Traverse. Above us rear sundry weird flakes and horns of sandstone, the like of which I have never seen. Above that lot another long crack appears – a very difficult move, with a prospect of a 50-ft. fall before Oliver could hold me.

'We end our fourth day sleeping on a ledge we call Hanging Garden.

TUESDAY. 'An easy traverse takes us slap into the middle of the North Wall. The butchering wind is again gale force.

'On I go up the Giant Steps, then crawl right inside a two-foot cleft, horizontal on my stomach. We call it The Vice.

WEDNESDAY. 'I feel it has to be the summit today. The overhang of the North Wall broods colossally over me. Not that way. So I edge up to the Guillotine, a terribly precarious 15 ft. long, 8 inch thick blade of sandstone, I have to stand on.

'I take a metal bolt kit out of my pocket delicately as a pickpocket, hardly daring to be alive, still less move on the flake lest it hear me.

'I try to insert a bolt in the rock above me – and then it happens. The Bolt-holder – without which no bolts can be inserted at all – breaks under my hammer.

'I am overcome with weakness and relief, because my hammer has made the decision for me. The climb cannot go on. Then I hear a curious croaking voice like Poe's raven, or a witch, and for one moment I wonder whether it's a greeting from the devil or death.

'Now, I do not know how, I go on without the bolts. I somehow find new strength and resolve, fist-jamming up the first cracks, picture railing steel hooks over the edges of small flakes. The hardest leading of my life; I have never known I could climb so hard on so little. I reach Thank God Ledge, invisible from below, and then up and over the top and Oliver and I sleep foodless but content.'

St. John's Head had already been climbed in 1969 for television.

The Old Man of Hoy is 2 miles south of St. John's Head. According to Tom Patey:

'This well-known landmark in the Pentland Firth' (it's a good ten miles from it) 'provided a 6-hour climb on 18th July, 1966, two days having been previously spent in reconnaissance and roping the climb as far as the top of the second pitch. The route followed the landward face of the pinnacle, which was denuded nearly a century ago by the collapse of a gigantic second leg which spanned an archway and is shown on prints of the early nineteenth century. This may account for the very unreliable nature of the rock as far as the 300-ft. contour, although we have no first-hand information regarding the south and seaward faces, both of which should provide equally spectacular lines.' (Climbed for television by J. Brown and Ian MacNaught-Davis.)

'The long second pitch of 100 ft. overhangs a total of 15 ft. throughout its length and was climbed entirely by artificial methods, although much of the pitch might have gone free had the rock been in any way trustworthy. The remaining 350 ft. was entirely free climbing and very spectacular. Most of the pitches overhang and the route spirals slightly, so that doubled ropes should be fixed in position during the ascent, to avoid bottomless abseils!

'At the end of the boulder ridge linking the Old Man to the mainland climb a shattered pillar, at the top of which is a large ledge on the S.E. corner (70 ft.). Tension-traverse right to gain the foot of a 100 ft. crack (20 ft.) and climb the crack using 'bing bongs' or wooden wedges throughout, passing roofs at 30 ft. and again at 60 ft. Step right at the top into a triangular alcove (100 ft.). Step right and move back left over loose easy ledges to regain the crack line, which follow for 25 ft. to a large ledge (50 ft.). Near the right-hand end of the ledge, climb a few feet then traverse delicately leftwards to another ledge. Climb the chimney in the corner, then wriggle along a horizontal ledge to the right until easy ledges lead to a grassy slope below the Terminal Crack. Belay 20 ft. up the crack at a better ledge (150 ft.).

'Climb the Terminal Crack, which is both strenuous and sensational, but the rock is now excellent and the standard no more than average Very Severe (70 ft.).'

North of St. John's Head one mile is the Kame of Hoy, a headland 952 ft. high. It, and the valley of the Kame with its wonderful echo, are worth a visit.

ROUSAY

Blotchnie Field (821 ft.)

There is a steamer service on Mondays and Saturdays from Kirkwall, and a daily mail boat service from Tingwall on the Mainland. Boats may be hired from M. Flaws. Tel. Wyre 203. Cars may be hired on Rousay.

Apart from Blotchnie Field there is ample hill-walking to be had on this island. Between Scarba Head and Sacquoy Head on the northwest the cliffs are around 400 ft. high with fine geos, stacks, caves, and three gloups. From the top of Blotchnie Field the high rock of Foula can be seen 75 miles away.

Rousay has Midhowe Chambered Cairn and other interesting antiquarian remains. On the neighbouring Egilsay is a famous church and Round Tower.

Rousay is separated from Mainland by Eynhallow Sound. Eynhallow island is a bird sanctuary. Thirty-three species of birds nest regularly on it and many others come as visitors. Seals forgather here in large numbers. It is the Holy Island of the Norse settlers of the Orkneys. Usually surrounded by turbulent waters, the Burgar Roost and the Cutlar Roost, it is also known as the vanishing island that could often be seen but never reached. The enchantment could be dispelled if a man kept his eyes fixed on the island and a knife clasped in his hand.

WESTRAY

Fittay Hill (557 ft.)

Steamers run from Kirkwall on Wednesdays and Saturdays, and to Kirkwall on Mondays and Thursdays. On Fridays there is a 'round the isles' trip. Loganair run a service twice a week from Kirkwall. Boats may be hired from W. L. Seatter, Mount Pleasant, Pierowall, Tel. Westray 29, and others. Cars may be hired in Pierowall.

The northern and western sides of the island are hilly, and the sea-cliffs, though not so high as some others in the Orkneys, are impressive. On the south side of the Bay of Skaill the Hole O'Rowe penetrates the headland. The cliff can be descended to see the waves burst and foam up through the hole whilst the spent water cascades back into the bay.

Two miles from the medieval ruin of Noltland Castle on the west coast is 'Gentleman's Ha' ' supposed to have been used by Jacobite outlaws.

THE SHETLAND ISLANDS

Mainland, Bressay, Noss, Mousa, Foula, Fair Isle and Unst.

Maps: One-inch O.S. Seventh Series, sheets 1, 3 and 4.
Half-inch Bartholomew, sheet 62.
Quarter-inch Geological Survey, sheets 1 and 2.

Fifty miles of sea separate the nearest points of Orkney and Shetland. Lerwick is farther north than the southernmost tip of Greenland and 180 miles north of Aberdeen.

There are hotels at Lerwick, Scalloway, Spiggie, Hillswick and Baltasound, but on the whole the Shetlands are not geared to tourism as is Orkney. Tom Weir said – 'We carried camping kit and so avoided being bedless in Lerwick because there was no accommodation to be found (in August). The few hotels and boarding-houses in the "Tourist Pamphlet" were full, and so were other places we tried.'

The Shetlands have more granite in their make-up than the Orkneys and for this reason may be more attractive to climbers of the old school The great variety of geological formations may be seen at the numerous cliff sections. The Noup of Noss is principally sandstones. The cliffs at Ronas Voe, north-west of the Mainland are a coarse, friable red granite. The serrated reefs and knife-edged pinnacles of Yell's west coast are weathered and tilted masses of mica schist. Many of the stacks, skerries and headlands are huge blocks of basalt or porphry.

There are more than 100 islands in the group, of which about 20 are inhabited.

Snowy owls have recently started to breed on Fetla – supposed to be the first island to be colonised by Vikings. The bird has never before been recorded so far south. Usually they breed on the Arctic Tundra of North Scandanavia, North Siberia, North America and Greenland.

MAINLAND

Ronas Hill (1475 ft.) in the north.
Bonxa Hill (960 ft.) in the south.

The hills on this island, as on the others in the archipelago are mostly low, smoothly sloping, and covered with rough grass and heather.

Ronas Hill is the highest point in the Shetlands. The view from it is immense. South from it across Ronas Voe is a promontory called the Ness of Hillswick. Lying just off this to the south-west is the Drongs, a great perpendicular rock pillar 100 ft. high. It and the precipitous cliffs around the Ness are of brilliant variegated colours. There are grotesquely interesting stacks, caves and crags in the area. On the opposite of the little Bay of Sandwick – not to be confused with West Sandwick, which is east, on Yell – are the bright red heads of Grocken with some fine teeth.

Fitful Head (928 ft.) is also of interest. Tom Weir writes:

'I explored Fitful Head and saw scope for great climbing of considerable height and exposure, from sea to summit in places; not many birds either.' It was mentioned by another author, Sir Walter Scott, in his *Pirate*. Five miles to the south-east is Sumburgh Head, where there are the excavated dwellings of early man – Jarlshof, a Pictish village and an airport.

Otherwise for good cliff and stack climbing the northern end of the island is the most promising. To those who don't carry expansion bolts the geological map will here again be the best guide.

Dr. Robert Cowie in his *Shetland: Descriptive and Historical*, 1871 describes a boat trip – 'which shows the traveller such an extent of scenery with little fatigue'. Starting by – 'descending the Voe of Bigster [through the Firth and down Sandsound Voe] through the Bay of Scalloway, availing when possible of the shelter of its islands. Sailing up the harbour of Scalloway and down that fine stretch of land-encompassed water termed Cliff Sound, rounding the Head of Ireland and reaching Bigton. A 60-mile journey has thus been ac-

complished through land-locked voes and bays and sounds, inter-
rupted by only two short portages' – canoeists take note.

BRESSAY

Ward of Bressay (742 ft.)

This island which is close to Lerwick has a frequent ferry service
throughout weekdays and also on Sunday. Boat hires can be arranged
through W. Kirkpatrick at Lerwick Pier.

The cave near the southern promontory, which is only accessible
by boat, is worth a visit. The entrance is a symmetrical archway wide
enough to admit several boats abreast. Here the water is very clear
and deep, the colours on the roof and walls remarkable for brilliance
and variety. Beyond the narrows is a spacious hall with stalagtites
hanging from the ceiling (take a torch). It is possible to penetrate
beyond for a considerable distance.

The rock forms, especially the Giant's Leg in the region of the
promontory of the Bard are worth inspecting.

NOSS

Noup of Ness (592 ft.)

The island is a nature reserve.

Access on Sundays, Mondays and Thursdays only. Ferry to
Bressay, then bus or car. The Warden provides boat transport across
Noss Sound. Boat hire – Kirkpatrick, Lerwick Pier.

From the summit of the Noup to the sea is a vertical drop. On the
cliff are thousands of gannets, guillemots, puffins, fulmars, shags, etc.
The Holm of Noss is a stack 160 ft. high a short distance south of the
Noup and separated from the cliff by a 65 ft. gap. It was climbed by
an engineer who fixed the stakes holding ropes which spanned the
gap, on which ran a box cradle. The said engineer is supposed to
have fallen and been drowned in his attempt to return.

MOUSA

The Hamars (140 ft.)

Boat hire from the Sandwick about half-way down the east coast between Lerwick and Sumburgh Head. P. Smith, St. Albem. Tel. Sandwick 217.

The finest and best preserved broch in existence is to be seen here.

PAPA STOUR (The Priest's Big Island)

Virda Field (288 ft.)

Mail boat on Mondays, Wednesdays and Fridays from Sandness.

Though only two miles across a complete circuition of the island takes many hours of hard going up and down. It has the finest set of sea caves in Britain, not to mention the many interesting skerries, stacks and voes of its coast.

FOULA

The Sneu, (1372 ft.
Hamnafeld (1126 ft.)

Mail boat between Foula and Walls on Mondays. It leaves Foula about mid-day and Walls during the evening. Enquire locally or telephone Foula 1.

Excursion to Foula on Mondays operated by H. Smith, Greenbank, Berry Road, Scalloway. Tel 201. Hires by arrangement with H. Smith. Charge £24 per day return (1970).

The best landing on the island is at a little islet exactly in the middle of the eastern coast. The western part of Foula is occupied by five conical peaks as steep as they are high. The habitations are confined to the eastern half, a level plain running from end to end. On top of Hamnafeld is a narrow chimney, the Lum of Liorafeld, reputed to go down into Hell.

The white-tailed eagle used to breed on the cliffs.

Tom Weir says in the *Scottish Field*:

'Soberlie Hill is the most dramatic climb you can do on Foula, because the edge of Soberlie is a cliff, rising with every foot of ascent until you land on North Bank leading to the celebrated Kame, greatest precipice of Foula. It presents itself dramatically. You climb up a steep ridge linked to the backbone of the island, then suddenly you find yourself overlooking nothing, just a vertical plunge of 1250 ft., more frightening than anything on St. Kilda, in my opinion.

Conachair of St. Kilda is tame by comparison. I know, because I have climbed down the St. Kilda cliff, but I could not do the same on Foula as the face is too sheer. I did climb down a little bit, and my imagination reeled at the thought of a slip down past the layers of gliding fulmars and quick whirring puffins and kittiwakes that looked about the size of butterflies. I have seen no other sea-cliff to compare with the Kame, especially with the mists of approaching storm heightening its effect above the wrinkles of the silver sea. No wonder the wind which screams across the Atlantic is deflected with such terrible force when it meets this buffer of cliff.

'Although it was July, we wore gloves, such was the cold on top of the Sneug at 1373 ft., second highest hill in the Shetlands. In another mile we were blown across the Brustins and down the ridge of Hamnafeld, exhilarated at such a fast and effortless descent.

'The most secret place in the western cliffs, though, is the Sneck of the Smallie, where the Wick of Mucklabeg is cleft by a mighty chimney a veritable keyhole leading underground until all that is visible of the sky is a narrow slit 200 ft. over your head. Down there you share your subterranean passage with thousands of puffins and green-eyed shags who turn reptilian heads at you as you emerge. Here you are ringed completely by sea cliffs. There is a sensational route out to the tops by a wild-fowlers' gangway traversing the face of the Afshins to Wester Head, which is the nearest point to the Fareos Islands and Iceland, beyond which lie the "West Ice", as the Shetland fishermen call the Greenland seas.

'From the summit of the Sneug, the highest hilltop of Foula, there is a magnificent view of the whole west coast of Shetlands and several of the Orkney islands.'

FAIR ISLE

Ward Hill (712 ft.)

A bird observatory was founded in 1949 by G. Waterston. The island was acquired by the National Trust for Scotland in 1964.

ACCESS:
Mail boat operated between Grutness (Sumburgh) and Fair Isle on Tuesdays and Fridays. Loganair service from Orkney. Boat hire from J. Stout, Leogh, Fair Isle. Tel. Fair Isle 13.

Accommodation is available in the hostel. It may be used by other than ornithologists when there is room to spare. Permission to stay may be obtained from the Warden. The headquarters of the Bird Observatory Trust are at 17 India Street, Edinburgh.

The island, which is 24 miles north of Sumburgh Head, is mostly girt with formidable precipices. The landing at, and the ascent from the Sheep Rock, is quite a tricky operation at any time. The rock is reputedly not good for climbing.

About 300 species of birds have been noted on the island, which has its own colonies of Great and Arctic Skuas.

UNST

Hermaness Hill (657 ft.)
Saxa Vord (935 ft.)

There is a service on alternate days approximately, by a route mostly overland, from Lerwick. Hires arranged at other times through D. Johnston, Moreview, Gutcher, Yell. Tel. Gutcher 202.

The hills are in the extreme north; Hermaness Hill to the west and Saxa Vord to the east of Burra Firth. A mile north-west is Muckle Flugga, the northernmost bit of Britain, Lat. 60° 51' north. A stairway has been cut in the rock up to the famous lighthouse, but many more 'sporting' ways to it could be found.

Beyond lies Tir nan Og, the last island for climbers and Aurora Polaris, the curtain across the end of the world.

41. The Hole o'Rowe. Orkney.

42. St. John's Head, Hoy.

43. Cliffs south of the Bay of Skaill.

44. The Old Man of Hoy. I. Clough using new techniques.

REFERENCES

A Vertebrate Fauna of the Shetland Islands, A. M. Evans and T. E. Buckley, Edinburgh, 1899.

The Birds of Shetland, H. L. Saxby, Edinburgh.

The Behaviour, Breeding and Food Ecology of the Snowy Owl, Nyctea Scandioca, 'Ibis' 99, 419, to 492.

The Land of the Loon, G. K. Yeates, London, 1951.

North Sea Pilot, Part I.

Report of the Royal Commission on Ancient and Historical Monuments (Orkney and Shetlands).

Ancient Monuments, VI, H.M.S.O.

Rambles of a Geologist, Hugh Millar, 1858.

The Islands of Scotland, Hugh MacDiarmid, 1939. Batsford.

The Pirate. Sir Walter Scott.

Orkney, the Magnetic North, J. Gunn, 1932, Nelson.

Sundry ornithological works: R. Perry, N. Rankin and others.

Sundry fictional works: E. Linklater.

Sundry poetical works: E. Muir.

Voyage, Christopher North.

The *Sunday Telegraph* – The Ascent of St. John's Head by Anthony Greenbank and E. Ward Drummond, 16th and 23rd July, 1970.

The Scottish Mountaineering Club Journal, Vol. 29, p. 322.

9

The Bass Rock, Isle of May

BASS ROCK (313 ft. high).

Maps: One-inch O.S., Seventh Series, sheet 56.
Half-inch Bartholomew, sheet 46.

Permission to land must be sought from the proprietors, the family of Dalrymple of North Berwick. Without the key it is impossible to reach the upper part of the island.

Standing prominently in the North Sea, near the eastern entrance to the Firth of Forth and 1½ miles directly out from Tantallon Castle, the Bass Rock rising precipitously from the water is a conspicuous object for many miles around. The cliffs plunge straight into the sea on all sides except the south-east, where it slopes steeply down to a rocky promontory on one or other side of which a landing may be made, according to weather. A first impression is that it is no place for anything but birds.

In the face of such overwhelming forces the climber might well think better of attacking this gannet's stronghold of rubble and guano. By descending from the path just at the top of a long flight of steps which leads down to the foghorn, a short traverse to the right takes one to the top of a shallow gully. Descending this leads to a large terrace half way down the cliffs, from which one may traverse left or right. The rock is in fact so rotten that it comes away in lumps in your hand. There is, however, an iron chain which goes down the 'gully' and makes the descent safe. The rock – the innermost part of the old volcano – is granular greenstone or clinkerstone whose cross-joints make such good nesting ledges for myriads of birds and such bad material for climbing.

A cave runs right through the island at sea-level. About 170 yards long, it maintains a height of at least 20 ft. throughout. Harold Raeburn wrote about it in the *S.M.C. Journal*, Vol. IV, p. 324.

An official 'Climber of the Bass' used to be employed to catch gannets. A dish of them was sent annually to Queen Victoria. James VI was protector of the gannets. He put a penalty of £20 on taking a bird, but if the culprit couldn't pay he had to stay on the rock for a year when he probably had a surfeit.

Above the landing-place are the remains of an old fort. Other remains on the island include the ancient Cell of St. Baldred, half-way up the acclivity. Inside the old fortress, where once the Jacobites held out for three years against William III, the rare Tree or Bass Mallow is growing.

ISLE OF MAY (160 ft.)

Maps: One-inch O.S., Seventh Series, sheet 56.
Half-inch Bartholomew, sheet 46.

Isle of May lies in the entrance of the Firth of Forth about $4\frac{1}{2}$ miles from the Fife and 9 miles from the East Lothian coasts. It is $1\frac{1}{4}$ miles long and $\frac{1}{4}$ mile broad.

The best and cleanest rock – basalt and greenstone, but much more reliable than usual – is to be found on the south-west of the island around Pilgrim's Haven. These give a number of short climbs of between 15 and 50 ft. The main feature of the cove is an isolated pinnacle. It is about 80 ft. high and vertical on three sides. It has been climbed on its fourth side, the sea-facing ridge, to reach the start of which one has to swim, except at low tide. There are two tops, one climbed from the gap between by a slab, the other by a flake or a steep ridge. The outlook is sensational.

There is another fine stack at the south end. The lower north end is one of the most populous terneries in the country. In early summer this isle is a great nesting site for guillemots, puffins, cormorants, fulmars and eiders. Unlike the Bass Rock it has no gannets.

The island was a celebrated place of pilgrimage after St. Adrian, the first Bishop of St. Andrews, was murdered here in the ninth century by the Danes. A rich monastery existed, whose ruins may be seen near Kirk Haven in the south-east, and miracles were believed to have been wrought by drinking at the Pilgrim's Well, on the slope up from Pilgrim's Haven.

EPILOGUE

Now we seem to be faced with two questions. The first is – 'When is an island not an island?'

Stack climbing is unique, as unique as gritstone climbing, Trilachan Slab climbing, or hard ice climbing in Scotland. It is a specialist section of the sport of mountaineering, and its greatest exponent was Tom Patey. It is going to demand a guide-book to itself soon. What, one wonders, will be the editor's criterion for inclusion – height and or area, and does reaching the top by any means count as having 'done' it? (The crossing to the Stack of Handa was particularly hazardous, for instance, according to Tom Patey.) Then there should be a grading for difficulty of access and landing, and on the ascent, the amount of time spent in the middle air hanging from 'Jumars' and 'étriers'.

In this new area of exploration, ability and versatility in the use of modern appliances has triumphed. One of the arguments used to justify the tremendous risks and cost of space travel is its 'spin-off' – that the material developed for rocket nose cones is good for saucepans, for instance. The same arguments may be used in favour of the efforts of the climber-spaceman who does for mountaineering what the racing driver does for motor, or the test-pilot for aero engineering.

The second question is – 'When is a climb not a climb?'

The *Oxford English Dictionary* says that 'to climb' is 'to make way up' something: 'to mount'. But we talk about 'climbing down' nowadays. Can we therefore 'climb' sideways as well, and should there be a sideways climbing guide? It is beyond the scope of this work, but already exponents of 'the crab crawl' do up to 10,000 ft. of continuous V.S. traversing. It is done unroped, so that you can fall straight into the sea, across the generally sound rock on all sea cliffs between high and low water marks. The term was coined by Don Whillans who, when invited by Tom Patey to accompany him on the 8000 ft. girdle traverse of Craig Meaghaidh, replied:

'Look, mate, do you know what you want to do? You want to team up with a crab. It's got claws, walks sideways and it's got a thick 'ead. This isn't a climb, it's a bloody crab-crawl!'

But it offers great possibilities for spectacular cliff-top photography. If sensationalism is wanted in the presentation of our sport to the ever widening ever more static televiewing public, then this is the greatest advance in mountaineering, and we have a particular advantage in the British Isles with its rugged sea-girt shores. As was snow and ice technique, so will be evolved a technique for dealing with seaweed, slime and guano.

And so we do progress – or do we digress?

By reading the press or watching television you would imagine that climbing was all Super Severes done by superlative performers. Nobody likes to knock the image of desperate men in a desperate sport. We all like to bathe in a bit of reflected glory. The trouble begins when we begin to take the shadow for the substance: when we really start to believe in the myth we have created.

It is the nature of youth to push forward the boundaries of experience and this is good. For all of us, whatever way we take it, there must always be that element of the uncertain in our sport of climbing to make it worthwhile; and that element is always present in the islands. Experience seems to teach us though, that we are more likely to find treasure by going up – to the top of Ben More say, than sideways or down – even to the bottom of Tobermory Bay.

REFERENCES

Report of Royal Commission on Ancient and Historical Monuments (*East Lothian*, Vol. 1).

The Bass Rock, Its Civil and Ecclesiastical History, Geology, Martyrology, Zoology and Botany, Hugh Miller and others. Published in 1848.

North Berwick and its Vicinity, G. Ferrier.

Old Mortality, Sir Walter Scott.

Mountain, Rocksport, The Climber, the *Sunday Times*, *Sunday Telegraph* and similar periodicals.

The *Scottish Mountaineering Club Journal*:
    Vol. 19, p. 25, The Bass Rock by W. Douglas.
        4, p. 342, Cave on Bass by H. Raeburn.
       20, p, 167, Bass Rock and Isle of May by W. Ross Maclean.
       21, p. 53, Isle of May by H. W. Turnbull.

The privilege of access

All land in the Highlands, except a minute urban fraction, is owned or tenanted by people who either try to earn a living from it or give employment. No man who owns land can survive financially today unless he turns his land to some good use. His hill lands are under sheep, cattle, deer, grouse and trees. He employs shepherds, cattlemen, stalkers, gillies, gamekeepers, ponymen and others to maintain the stock, tracks, gates, fences, houses, bothies and plantations. The living environment that he helps to maintain attracts visitors in large numbers.

Visitors, whether tourists, walkers, campers or climbers can injure Highland life by carelessness. The management and culling of livestock, and the money-earning sports of stalking and grouse-shooting, require a seasonal control of access.

Deer-stalking. The normal season is from 1 September to 20 October, when stag culling ends. Hinds are culled from then until 15 February.

Grouse-shooting. Grouse are shot from 12 August to 10 December.

The passage of a walker can clear a glen of its deer, and a moor of its grouse, for that day. The deer may not move back for weeks unless driven by weather, thus the walker may disrupt a season's stalking. While stalking is for many a sport like mountaineering, for others who run hill farms the venison exports are essential to keep marginal enterprises solvent. Therefore, before taking to the hills or to grouse moors, inquire at the estate office if you know where it is, or at the nearest farmhouse, or ask the local owner or keeper, if deer are to be stalked or grouse shot that day. The courtesy will be greatly appreciated. An alternative route may be offered to you should the need arise.

The problem of access to deer forests or grouse moors in late summer and autumn may be avoided if you go instead to mountain ranges held by the National Trust for Scotland in Arran, Ben Lawers, Glencoe, Kintail and Torridon.

Sheep. In the lambing months of April and May, take no dog on to sheep grazings. Pregnant ewes can suffer injury if forced to run. If a sheep is found on its back, approach quietly, place it on its feet gently, and stand by until it can move steadily. Do not try to 'rescue' sheep apparently stuck on ledges: if approached by a stranger they may jump off and fall to their death. Instead, report to the farmer.

Fire and litter. Great damage to plants, trees, birds and animals is done annually in the Highlands by fire, and to mammals by litter. It is urgently important that everyone should observe the Country Code:

Guard against all risk of fire
Fasten all gates
Keep dogs under proper control
Keep to the paths across farm land
Avoid damaging fences, hedges and walls
Leave no litter - take it home
Safeguard water supplies
Protect wildlife, wild plants and trees
Go carefully on country roads
Respect the life of the countryside

Amendment 1976

ACCESS

Access has changed so radically (MacBraynes alter almost every one of their services annually) that readers are advised always to refer to current time-tables.

P. 16   Delete 'Car'.   Read 'Ferry services -'.   For 'Fairlie' read 'Largs and Wemyss Bay'.
Islay and Jura are served from Kintyre.

25   (Arran) There is no ferry from Fairlie to Brodick.

43   (Great Cumbrae) Ferry service from Largs only.

49   (Islay) Ferry from Kennacraig, Western Ferries;
Managing Agents - Harrisons (Clyde) Ltd.
16 Woodside Crescent, Glasgow.
Telephone: 041-332-9766

50   (Jura) From Port Askaig to Feolin only.

57   (Colonsay) from Oban.

61   (Mull) from Oban to Craignure, from Lochaline to Fishnish, and from Mingary (Ardnamurchan) to Tobermory (passenger only).

71   (Iona)
from Oban - passenger service, including close view of Staffa. Fionnphort - Iona (passenger), via Oban-Craignure (car ferry). No service from Fort William.

87   (Eigg) service from Arisaig (Murdo Grant, Hotel, Arisaig. Telephone 224).

92   (Muck) from Mallaig (MacBraynes), as well as service from Arisaig.

99   (North Lewis) from Ullapool to Stornoway.

119   (North Uist) from Uig, Skye to Lochmaddy.   The service is from Oban, not Mallaig to Lochboisdale.

122　(South Uist)　from Oban to Lochboisdale.

127　(Barra)　from Oban to Castlebay.

147　The company plying to the Orkneys and Shetlands is:
P. & O. Ferries, North of Scotland Orkney and Shetland Shipping Company Limited, Matthew's Quay, Aberdeen AB9 8DL. Telephone 0224 29101. They also have offices at Scrabster, Kirkwall and Lerwick.

148　Orkney Mainland - by sea from Scrabster to Stromness (2 hrs) or from Aberdeen to Kirkwall (11 hrs). Local air connections from Wick to Kirkwall.

150　An alternative way of reaching Hoy, apart from the route by Orkney Mainland, is by coal tender from Scrabster.

154　Westray may be reached by boat from Rousay, or from Orkney Mainland.

155　The Shetland Islands are reached by air from Abbotsinch to Sumburgh, 27 miles south of Lerwick; by air from Kirkwall in Orkney; or by boat from Aberdeen or Leith to Lerwick.

158　Papa Stour may be reached by boat from Melby, Shetland Mainland.

160　Unst - by the inter-island steamer from Lerwick, or by boat from Yell.

ADDENDA

P. 7　Illustrations

No. 7　Gylen, not Gylan

No. 8　Ellen, not Ellan

No. 10　Corrievrekan, not Corrievrachen

P. 8　No. 36　Stac an Armin, not Stac Lee

15　The Scottish Islands in order of height. Skye's highest top is now 3257 ft. (993 metres) - Munro's Tables, Revised Edition by J. C. Donaldson.

16　Eriskay, not Eriska
Garvelloch, not Garvellach

170

Flannan Mor, not Flannan Mar

17   3rd para. W. H. Murray's <u>Islands of Western Scotland</u>
(Eyre Methuen) is to be recommended as an up to date guide.

19   Oronsay has yielded the earliest carbon date - 3800
B. C. - of early man in the Hebrides.

20   For 'house mouse' read 'field mouse'. It may be pre-
Ice Age (Boyd & Darling).
11th line from bottom: read 'kittiwake' with a small 'k'.

22   The stone forts with timber frames have been carbon
dated 6th Century B. C.

26   General. 1st para. 2nd last line: schists, not shists.

39   Holy Island is now the the property of the Univer-
sities Federation for Animal Welfare, who are running a
farmhouse on the island as a field study centre for schools and
college parties. Since Soay sheep are resident along with the
wild white goats, the naturalists may have difficulty separating
them, in the Biblical or any other sense.

48   Last para. 4th and 8th lines - Tayvallich, not Tayviallich.
Photograph: Gylen Castle

49   Photograph: Port Ellen

51   Lines 2 and 3 and 2nd last - Feolin, not Feoline

50   Jura. Beinn Shiantaidh (2477)

51   As p. 50

52   Line 7: Feolin
Line 10: Shiantaidh
5th para, 3rd line: Britain
3rd last para. The Norse name for Jura was Dyr Öe.
Last para, (twice): Corrievreckan

53   Last para, 2nd line: Corrievreckan

55   Garvelloch Isles. Garbh Eileach

56   Lines 1, 4 and 6 and 1st line of 4th para -
Garbh Eileach
Line 4 and 1st line of 6th para - Eileach an Naoimh. Eileach

means a rock or skerry rather than an island.
Last para, W. D. Simpson dates the chapel as 9th century.
The beehive cells may be 7th century.

61 3rd para. It was St. Molvag who evangelised Lismore and founded his monastry there in 561 - 564, when St. Columba was doing likewise in Iona.

62 5th para. Rum, not Rhum

63 3rd para. Rum, not Rhum
4th para, Beinn Dearg, not Beinn Bearg

66 Last para, rhyolites

68 2nd para, Daniel
Coast. The pink granite cliffs are 100 feet high. There is no climbing that would require the use of a rope.

69 Last para, Corylus (hazel), Quercus (oak)

71 Eilean Shona. Following the backbone of the island makes a splendid, long expedition hardly to be encompassed in one strenuous day.

72 3rd para, Columba arrived in 563

73 2nd last para, Corrievreckan

74 References. See also McNab's book on Mull.

87 2nd para, Pabay, not Pabbay
Eigg. Beinn Bhuidhe
2nd last para. Delete Rhu and the reference to Roddie Campbell and the The Factor, Eigg. Substitute M. Grant, the Hotel, Arisaig ('phone 224).

91 3rd last para, 1st and 2nd last lines; Beinn Bhuidhe

100 1st para. Some say Pigmy's Isle. Better to call it Luchruban. W. H. Murray says the climb to the summit is dead easy. The researchers of the 17th century thought differently.
The chessmen were found at Camus Uig in the Ardriol sands. (Reference on p. 103).

121 Photograph. Stac an Armin, not Stac Lee

122 2nd para, 5th line; Rossinish

128   2nd last para. The castle is repaired and occupied.

140   St. Kilda: Boreray, not Bororay

NEW CLIMBS

P. 35   Arran.   Beinn Nuis.   The steep slabs (which merge into a prow) to the right of the Beinn Nuis Chimney have been climbed by a route called Right On 610 ft. V.S. & A2 described in the S.M.C.J. 1971.

P. 36   Arran. Beinn Tarsuinn. Meadow Face. Blinder 450 ft. Very Severe by J. Crawford and W. Skidmore features in the 1972 Scottish Mountaineering Club Journal both as a long article and in detail as a rock route.

   In the same issue details are given of Klepth on Cioch na h'Oighe and three new routes on the lower slabs of Caisteal Abhail, where yet another route, Ourpolhode, may be found, described in the 1973 Journal.

P. 50   Islay.   Mull of Oa.   The South Ridge of Beinn Mhor 400 ft.   Very Severe by R. Cuthbert and N. Tennent, starts at the extreme southernmost tip of the island on its west side. The Dun Athad Arête provides an easy scramble and fine views of the surrounding cliffs below the American Monument.

P. 88   Eigg.   An Sguir.   The Nose 300 ft.   Very Severe and A3 by L. Boulton and K. Jones follows a direct line up the green fluted overhanging eastern nose of the Sguir. The start is at a leftward slanting groove, directly beneath the central overhanging section, where a thin crack is climbed in a steep wall past a small overhang.

P. 101   Lewis. Uig. Mealisval.   Creagan Thealastail.   The Porker 300 ft. Severe, lies on the central buttress. A recess near the middle is bounded on the right by overlapping slabs. The climb starts at a ramp leading rightwards and follows the slabs. (Defaced by an arrow).

P. 104   Lewis. Sgoran Dubh Theinneasbhal. Flannan. Very Severe, follows a line by No. 1 Rib. No height is given in the 1973 Scottish Mountaineering Club Journal, but Nosferatu a 620 feet Very Severe by B. Clarke and K. Tremain must be one of the longest routes on the island. Start to the right of the South Buttress Route. Scramble 20 ft. to belay peg below a slab. Traverse right, climb wall, then a slab and groove to a niche on an arête. The route traverses right under an overhang.

P. 105   Creag Dubh Dhibadail. Two routes are given in the 1971 Scottish Mountaineering Club Journal. Via Valtos 500 ft. Very Severe and A3, by A. Ewing and W. Sproul is the crack line on the left hand side of the face. It is ascended directly with occasional excursions onto the flanking walls.
Solitude 570 ft. Very Severe by J. Ball and M. Reeves is the right hand of two cracks flanking the central wall.

P. 105   Lewis. Suainaval. Sron ri Gaoith has cliffs 300 - 400 feet high offering climbs in the middle grades, according to G. M. Wallace.

P. 105   Harris. Ben Luskentyre on the south side of West Loch Tarbet has some rock faces broken by terraces overlooking the loch. K. V. Crocket found the climbing good, reminiscent of the Etive Slabs. A rising traverse, which he did with Miss K. Simpson was pleasantly severe. The editor who recently tried the slabs whilst waiting for the boat, was not so impressed.

P. 108   Lewis. Creag Mo. Footpad 350 ft. B. Clarke and J. Macdougall goes up steep rock to the right of the Amphitheatre. Below and right to the Amphitheatre is an arete of white slabby rock: scramble up steep grass and belay under small overhang. Step left and climb grooved arête, then wall to terrace below Amphitheatre. Descend slabby grooves and grass diagonally right. Climb successively a groove to a pedestal, a crack, a chimney, then a groove, and so to the top.

MAPS

The 1:50,000 Ordnance Survey Maps of Scotland, based on a re-survey will be numbered 1 to 85. The heights of mountains shown on these maps (pp. 15 & 16) may differ by a few feet from those shown on the old ones.

The islands covered and the sheet numbers are as follows:

Page 25	Arran	Sheet No.	69
49	Islay		60
50	Jura		61
56	Colonsay		61
61	Mull		47, 48
70	Ulva		47
72	Iona		48
73	Treshnish		47
75	Rum		39
87	Eigg		39
99	N. Lewis		8
106	Harris		13
	- Tarbet		14
119	N. Uist		18
121	Benbecula		22
122	S. Uist		22, 31
127	Barra		31
148	Orkney, N. Isles		5
	Mainland		6
	Hoy, Ronaldsay		7
155	Shetland, Yell & Unst		1
	N. E. Mainland		2

CAMPING

Regulations and conditions for camping have been made and changed on certain islands - Colonsay for instance. Inquiries should be made, where ever possible, to factors and landowners.

INDEX